Kitchen-Table Systematic Theology for Kids, A 52-Week Family Devotional

10-Minute Family Worship & Discipleship for Kids 8-12 with Stories, Prayer Prompts, Discussion Questions, and Parent Notes

Matthew R. Caldwell

Contents

Introduction

Welcome to the Kitchen Table

If you are holding this book, you probably have a deep desire to pass on your faith to your kids. You want them to know who God is, not just as a word they hear on Sundays, but as the foundation of their lives. You want them to know the *truth*, solid, historic, beautiful truth, in a world that feels increasingly confusing.

But if you are like most parents, you also feel two other things: **busy** and **unqualified**.

Maybe you didn't go to seminary. Maybe you feel like you barely understand theology yourself. Or maybe you just look at your family calendar, packed with soccer practice, homework, laundry, and exhaustion, and wonder, *When do we have time for a theology class?*

Here is the good news: **You don't need to be a theologian to teach your kids about God. You just need to be their parent.**

Discipleship doesn't happen in a lecture hall. It happens at the kitchen table. It happens in the car on the way to practice. It happens in the five minutes before bed. It happens in the messy, loud, real moments of life.

Why This Book Exists

We wrote this book to be the bridge between "deep theology" and "real life."

Most resources for kids fall into one of two traps. Either they are too fluffy (giving kids "be nice" moral lessons without any deep truth), or they are too heavy (giving kids dry academic lectures that feel like homework instead of hope).

This book walks a different path. We believe kids ages 8–12 are capable of understanding profound truths if we explain them simply. We believe they *need* to know about the Trinity, Justification, the Holy Spirit, and the End Times, not just to pass a test, but to navigate their fears, their friendships, and their futures.

The Benefit: Roots for the Storm

What you are building with this book is **resilience**. When your child understands *who God is* (Theology) and *who they are* (Identity), they have an anchor.

- When they feel lonely, the doctrine of the **Church** gives them belonging.

- When they mess up, the doctrine of **Justification** gives them peace.

- When they are scared, the doctrine of **Providence** gives them courage.

This book is designed to help you plant those roots without overwhelming your schedule. It is built for the parents who want depth but need a plan that works when life gets messy.

The Roadmap: A Year of Building Roots

Systematic theology sounds intimidating, but it is simply a map of who God is. We have broken this map into six clear parts. You don't have to tackle them all at once, just take it one week at a time.

Part 1: The Foundations (Weeks 1–6)

- **What it covers:** The Bible, Truth, and how we know God. **Why it matters:** We live in a world of "my truth" and "your truth." This section gives your kids a solid place to stand. **The Win:** Your child will trust the Bible as their compass, not just a dusty book.

Part 2: God the Father (Weeks 7–15)

- **What it covers:** The Trinity, God's Attributes (like Holiness and Love), and Creation. **Why it matters:** Small views of God lead to big fears. A big, robust view of God creates a safe harbor for a child's heart. **The Win:** Your child will feel safe knowing exactly *Who* is in charge of the universe.

Part 3: God the Son (Weeks 16–25)

- **What it covers:** Jesus, His life, humanity, divinity, death, and resurrection. **Why it matters:** Christianity isn't a list of rules; it's a Person. This section moves Jesus from a character in a storybook to the King of their lives. **The Win:** Your kids will move from knowing *about* Jesus to marveling *at* Him.

Part 4: Salvation & Identity (Weeks 26–36)

- **What it covers:** Sin, Grace, Forgiveness, Adoption, and Union with Christ. **Why it matters:** Kids today are crushed by the pressure to perform. This section teaches them they are loved because of *whose* they are, not *how well* they do. **The Win:** Freedom from shame and performance anxiety.

Part 5: The Holy Spirit & Growth (Weeks 37–44)

- **What it covers:** How we change, prayer, spiritual habits, and fighting temptation. **Why it matters:** Willpower runs out. Kids need to know they have a Helper inside them who empowers them to change. **The Win:** Practical tools for fighting temptation and growing in character from the inside out.

Part 6: The Church & Hope (Weeks 45–52)

- **What it covers:** Community, Mission, Suffering, and the End Times. **Why it matters:** Loneliness is an epidemic. This section invites them into a family and gives them a happy ending to look forward to. **The Win:** A sense of belonging and an unshakable hope for the future.

You can do this. Let's pull up a chair and get started.

How to Use This Book Without Overthinking It

You can make this work in a busy week. That's the point. This book is built like a family discipleship system, simple enough to run when you're tired, but deep enough to build real roots in your kids over time.

Who this book is for

- **Families with kids ages 8–12:** (and parents who want more than "be nice" devotionals).

- **Parents who want clarity:** You want clear theology, real-life application, and helpful scripts for conversations.

- **Homes that need a plan:** You need something that still works when life gets messy.

Who this book is NOT for (and that's okay)

- **Families looking for "hot air":** If you want a "one-minute inspirational thought" with no discussion, this isn't it.

- **Parents who want a textbook:** We do depth, but we keep it usable. If you want a heavy academic systematic theology tome, this isn't it.

The Three Lanes (What You're Actually Doing)

Every week runs on three lanes to help you teach with confidence:

1. Kid Lane (Short + Clear) This is the "Big Idea" in kid words. It includes simple definitions, the Anchor Verse, and key terms. It's designed to be read *to* or *by* your child.

2. Story Lane (The Hook) A realistic story that puts the theology into an everyday situation your kids recognize (school, sports, siblings, gaming). This bridges the gap between "truth" and "life."

3. Parent Lane (Your Confidence Booster) This is the "Secret Weapon" section at the end of the week. This is where you get:

- The doctrine explained clearly (so you understand it first). "Misunderstandings to avoid" (so you don't accidentally teach the wrong thing). Coaching phrases you can use in conversation. Extra Bible anchors and a short summary. *Note: You are not expected to be a theologian. You're expected to show up.*

The Weekly Rhythm (5 Short Blocks of Time)

Most families do 8–15 minutes a day. If that's not realistic, skip down to "Two Flexible Schedules."

Block 1: Kid Page (8–10 minutes) Read the Big Idea, Anchor Verse, and Key Words. (Tip: If your child is a confident reader, let them lead this part!)

- **Ask:** "What do you think this means?" **Goal:** Keep it moving. The goal is clarity, not a lecture.

Block 2: Story Page (10–12 minutes) Read the story out loud.

- **Ask:** "What was the hardest part for the character?" **Goal:** Let your kids react. Stories are where the buy-in happens.

Block 3: Talk-It-Out (10–15 minutes) This is your discussion day.

- **Use** the provided questions (Understand, Connect, Apply). **Use** the parent coaching prompts ("If your kid says…") if your child freezes, shrugs, or jokes their way out.

Block 4: Practice (5–10 minutes) One habit for the week.

- **Goal:** Small. Concrete. Repeatable. **Crucial:** Tie it to Jesus: "We do this because of what Jesus has done, not to earn anything."

Block 5: Parent Notes (10–20 minutes) This can be:

- **Parent-only reading** for your own growth (feel free to read this earlier in the week to feel prepared!), <u>OR</u> **read with the kids** (especially the "Teach-it-back" and "Memory" sections).

Two Flexible Schedules (Pick One)

Option A: The "Normal Week" Plan

- **Mon:** Block 1 – **Tue:** Block 2 – **Wed:** Block 3 – **Thu:** Block 4 – **Fri/Sat:** Block 5

Option B: The "We're Drowning" Plan (It still works!)

- **One day (e.g., Tuesday night):** Read Block 2 (Story) + Ask one question from Block 3 (Talk-It-Out). **Another day (e.g., Saturday morning):** Do Block 4 (Practice). **Parent:** Read Block 5 whenever you can (even in bed).

Remember: You are not failing if you don't do five days. Consistency over intensity.

How to Adjust by Age (8 vs 12)

If your child is closer to 8:

- Keep answers short. Let them draw their answer instead of explaining it. Choose one "Talk-It-Out" question (not all three).

If your child is closer to 12:

- Ask follow-ups: "Why do you think that?" "What would you do differently next time?" Have them summarize the Big Idea in their own words. Let them read parts aloud (kids often engage more when they lead).

If you have multiple kids:

- Ask the younger one first (quick answer). Then ask the older one for depth (why/how). Same content, different expectations.

What You Need (Minimal Setup)

- **A Bible** (any readable translation your family uses; the book uses CSB). **A pen/pencil. Optional:** A small notebook for "Family Notes" and prayer requests. *That's it.*

The "Discussion House Rules" (Highly Recommended)

Before you start Week 1, tell your kids these four rules. This keeps the tone safe, especially on sensitive topics. 1) **No mocking.** (We're learning, not performing). 2) **Questions are welcome. 3) "I don't know" is allowed. 4) We tell the truth, but we're kind.**

Troubleshooting

What if we miss a day (or a week)? Do not "make it up" by cramming unless you want to. Just restart the next day. Missed doing it on Day 1? Start with it on Day 2. Missed the whole week? Start the next week. Or repeat the same week, repetition is a feature, not a bug. **What if my kid is resistant?** Totally normal. Try these resets: "You don't have to talk a lot, just give me one thought." "Which part felt realistic? Which part felt fake?" "If this story was a movie, what would the lesson be?" "Let's do this for 7 minutes. Then we're done."

- **Remember:** If you get eye-rolls, you're not losing. You're planting.

The Two Knobs You Can Turn

Adjust these without breaking the system.

- **Knob #1: Time: Short on time?** Do the Story + one question. **More time?** Add Parent Notes + Teach-it-back.

- **Knob #2: Depth: Need simple?** Stay in Kid Words + Story. **Want deeper?** Use Parent Notes "misunderstandings" and Bible anchors. *You can run this book at Level 1 or Level 5 depending on the week.*

Success looks like:

- **Your child** starts noticing what's true and what's a lie. **Your home** has better language for fear, anger, shame, temptation, and hope. **Your kids** connect faith to real life. **You** stop panicking when your child asks a hard question. **You** keep showing up. **You**'re building something long-term.

- So you don't get discouraged, remember: **Success is not "my kids became little theologians overnight."**

Start Here (Week 1)

Pick a consistent time (even if it's short): after dinner, before bed, Saturday breakfast, or Sunday afternoon.

Then open to Week 1 and do Block 1. That's all.

Part 1: Foundations

Welcome to the beginning... where we lay the floor before we build the house. In this section, we're going to help your family get confident with the basics: **the Bible, truth, and how we know God**.

The goal isn't to turn your kids into mini-professors. The goal is to give them a **compass,** something steady to hold onto when the world is loud, confusing, and full of "my truth" and "your truth."

Each week in this part is a small, doable step. You'll work through the same simple rhythm... kid-friendly truth, a story that feels like real life, and just enough coaching to help you talk about it without freezing up. You don't need perfect energy for this.

You just need to **show up**, pull up a chair, and keep planting.

WEEK 1: WHAT IS THEOLOGY?

BLOCK 1: KID PAGE (Big Idea + Anchor Verse)

Big Idea: Theology is the study of God and what He has told us in the Bible. What we believe about God matters because it changes how we see ourselves, how we treat others, and how we make choices. We learn theology so we can know God better, love Him more, and have the right words to talk about Him.

Anchor Verse: John 17:3

In kid words: Knowing God the Father and Jesus the Son is what gives us true, forever life.

Key Words:

- **Theology:** The study of God. ('Theo' means God, and '-ology' means the study of).

- **Doctrine:** The specific truths and teachings we believe from the Bible.

More Bible places to look: Psalm 19:1–2; Jeremiah 9:23–24; Romans 11:33–36; Philippians 3:8; Colossians 2:2–3; 2 Peter 3:18; 1 John 5:20

BLOCK 2: STORY PAGE (Real Life Scenario)

Story Title: The New Kid at Lunch

Setting: Leo sat down at the cafeteria table across from Sam, a brand-new kid at his school.

Problem: They were trading snacks and talking about the weekend when Leo casually mentioned his church. Sam tilted his head and looked genuinely confused. 'Why do you believe in that God stuff anyway?' he asked. Leo froze. He stared down at his sandwich. His mind went totally blank when he tried to explain what he believed or why.

Choice moment: *I could just mumble something and quickly change the subject to video games,* Leo thought, *or I could admit it's hard to explain but try my best anyway.*

Small resolution: Leo took a deep breath. "It's kind of hard to put into words right now," he said. "I just know God is real and He loves us, but I'm still learning how to explain all the details." Sam shrugged, said, "Fair enough," and went back to his lunch. It wasn't a perfect speech, but Leo was proud he was honest.

Quick takeaway: Having the right words, which is what theology gives us, helps us understand our own faith and share it with others without freezing up.

<u>BLOCK 3: TALK-IT-OUT (Discussion + Coaching)</u>

1. **Understanding:** What does the word "theology" actually mean?

2. **Connection to life:** Tell me about a time you felt like Leo, where someone asked you a question about God (or the Bible) and your mind went completely blank.

3. **Application:** If you could learn the answer to one big question about God this year, what would it be?

If your kid says: "Theology sounds like boring schoolwork." **Try:** "It can sound like that! But it's really more like learning facts about your favorite athlete, musician, or hobby. When you love someone or something, you want to know everything about them. We study theology because we love God."

If your kid says: "I don't know what to ask about God." **Try:** "That's totally okay. We're going to learn a lot of new things together this year. For now, just think about what you would ask God if He was sitting right here at the table with us."

<u>BLOCK 4: PRACTICE (One Habit This Week)</u>

Habit: Start a "God Questions" list on the fridge.

When we'll do it: Whenever a confusing question pops into our heads during the week, we will write it down on the list instead of just forgetting about it.

What to watch for: Your child pausing to write a question on the list instead of getting frustrated or simply saying, 'I don't know.'

Prayer: Lord, thank You that You are big enough to handle all of our questions. Please help our family to learn about You, understand Your truth, and love You more this year. Amen.

<u>BLOCK 5: PARENT NOTES (The Secret Weapon)</u>

The Doctrine, Precisely Theology simply means "the study of God." While the word can sound intimidating or strictly academic, every Christian is a theologian. Everyone has thoughts, assumptions, and beliefs about who God is and how He operates in the world. The goal of discipleship is not to become a theologian, but to become a *good* theologian, one whose beliefs are accurately shaped by God's Word rather than by culture, feelings, or guesswork.

Good theology is the bedrock of a resilient faith. What we think about God shapes absolutely everything else about our lives. If a child views God as an angry cosmic policeman, they will hide from Him when they sin. If they view God as a genie, they will abandon Him when their prayers aren't answered exactly how they want. Proper theology anchors our kids in the objective truth of God's character.

Why It Matters

- **It protects against lies:** Kids will encounter a thousand different ideas about who God is from screens, friends, and the world; theology gives them a filter for truth.

- **It fuels worship:** We cannot truly love a God we do not know. Deep knowledge leads to deep affection.

- **It builds confidence:** Giving kids the vocabulary of faith helps them articulate what they believe when challenged, avoiding the panic Leo felt in the cafeteria.

Common Misunderstandings to Avoid

- **Misunderstanding:** Theology is only for pastors, scholars, and adults.

  - **Correction:** Theology is for everyone. If you have an opinion on who God is, you are doing theology. Kids are highly capable of understanding deep truths when given the right vocabulary.

- **Misunderstanding:** Knowing facts about God is the same as knowing God.

  - **Correction:** Theology is a means to an end, not the end itself. Information must lead to transformation and relationship.

- **Misunderstanding:** We shouldn't ask hard questions because it shows a lack of faith.

  - **Correction:** God welcomes honest questions. Theology is the active process of seeking those answers in His Word. Suppressing questions usually leads to doubt later on.

How to Answer Follow-Up Questions If they ask: "What if I get the theology wrong?" **Say:** "We all make mistakes, and we are all still learning. The beautiful thing is that God's grace covers our misunderstandings while the Holy Spirit slowly guides us into truth. We just keep reading the Bible and adjusting as we learn."

If they ask: "Why does it matter what I believe, as long as I'm a good person?" **Say:** "Because what we believe actually shapes who we become. We can't truly know what 'goodness' is without knowing the God who invented it."

If they ask: "How do we know our theology is the right one?" **Say:** "We measure everything against the Bible. That's why we study it together, so we can build our beliefs on what God actually says, not on our own guesses."

Extra Bible Anchors for Parents Proverbs 2:1–5; Romans 12:2; Colossians 1:9–10 John 17:3 , "And this is eternal life: that they may know you, the only true God, and the one you have sent, Jesus Christ." (CSB)

Teach-It-Back Prompt Sometime tomorrow, casually say: 'Hey, remind me what that big word theology means?' Have them explain it in their own words to you, a younger sibling, a grandparent, or even a pet.

MEMORY (One-Liner + Catechism Q/A)

One-Liner: Theology is studying what the Bible says so we can know and love God.

Optional Q&A: Q: What is theology? A: Theology is the study of God and His truth.

Notes:

WEEK 2: THE BIBLE: GOD'S WORD

BLOCK 1: KID PAGE (Big Idea + Anchor Verse)

Big Idea: The Bible is God's true message to us, written by human authors who were guided by the Holy Spirit. Because it comes directly from God, it is completely trustworthy and holds the ultimate authority over how we live. We read the Bible to discover who God is, what He has done, and how we can follow Him with our whole lives.

Anchor Verse: 2 Timothy 3:16

In kid words: Every single part of the Bible is breathed out by God and helps us learn how to live the right way.

Key Words:

- **Inspiration:** The way God the Holy Spirit guided human writers so that what they wrote was exactly what God wanted to say.

- **Authority:** The right to be in charge and make the rules. (Because God is in charge, His Word has the final say).

More Bible places to look: Psalm 119:105; Proverbs 30:5; Isaiah 40:8; Matthew 4:4; Hebrews 4:12; 2 Peter 1:20–21; James 1:22

BLOCK 2: STORY PAGE (Real Life Scenario)

Story Title: The Blank Worksheet

Setting: Maya sat at the kitchen table, staring at a math worksheet that was entirely blank except for her name at the top.

Problem: Her mom called from the living room, "Maya, did you finish your math homework yet? We need to leave for soccer practice in ten minutes!" Maya felt a knot in her stomach; she had spent the last thirty minutes building a tower out of erasers instead of doing her work. She knew if she told the truth, she would probably miss practice to finish it.

Choice moment: I could just yell "Yes!" and quickly stuff the blank paper into my backpack, or I could tell the truth and deal with the consequences.

Small resolution: Maya sighed and knocked over the eraser tower. "No, Mom," she called back, her voice shaking a little. "I got distracted and haven't started yet." Her mom walked in, looking disappointed, and told Maya she'd have to miss the first half of practice to finish. It wasn't fun, but Maya felt a weird sense of relief knowing she hadn't lied.

Quick takeaway: Because God's Word is completely true, we can trust that living truthfully is always better than hiding behind a lie.

BLOCK 3: TALK-IT-OUT (Discussion + Coaching)

1. **Understanding:** If someone asked you what it means that the Bible has "authority" over our lives, what would you tell them?

2. **Connection to life:** Tell me about a time you felt like Maya, where it would have been so much easier to tell a quick lie to stay out of trouble.

3. **Application:** What is one thing the Bible tells us to do that is sometimes hard for you to obey?

If your kid says: "But humans wrote the Bible, so couldn't they make mistakes?" **Try:** "Humans did write it, but God the Holy Spirit guided them perfectly. Think of it like a master musician playing a flute; the flute makes the sound, but the musician is the one creating the perfect song."

If your kid says: "The Bible is just a bunch of boring rules." **Try:** "It might feel like that sometimes! But God's rules are actually like guardrails on a mountain road. They aren't there to ruin our fun; they are there to keep us safe because God loves us."

BLOCK 4: PRACTICE (One Habit This Week)

Habit: Read one small part of the Bible together.

When we'll do it: Pick one morning or evening this week to read Psalm 23 together (maybe at the kitchen table or right before bed).

What to watch for: Your child noticing that the Bible talks about real, everyday feelings like fear and comfort, rather than just abstract rules.

Prayer: Lord, thank You for giving us the Bible so we can know exactly who You are and what You want for us. Please help us to trust Your Word and obey it, even when it is hard. Amen.

BLOCK 5: PARENT NOTES (The Secret Weapon)

The Doctrine, Precisely When we talk about the Bible, we are really focusing on three big ideas: inspiration, inerrancy, and authority. Historic Christianity teaches that the Bible is the inspired Word of God, meaning the Holy Spirit perfectly guided the human authors so that their very words were the words of God. Because it is breathed out by God, it is entirely true (inerrant) and serves as the ultimate rule for our faith and practice (authority).

We don't read the Bible merely as an ancient historical document or a collection of moral fables. We read it as the living, active voice of the Creator speaking to His creation. When the Bible speaks, God speaks. Therefore, submitting to the Bible is the exact same thing as submitting to God Himself.

Why It Matters

- **It gives us an objective standard:** In a world that tells kids to "follow their heart" or "create their own truth," the Bible provides a solid, unchanging foundation.

- **It reveals God's character:** We don't have to guess what God is like; He has explicitly shown us His justice, mercy, and love in the pages of Scripture.

- **It equips us for life:** The Bible contains everything we need to know for salvation and godly living, guiding us through complex real-world choices.

Common Misunderstandings to Avoid

- **Misunderstanding:** The Bible was dictated by God to human robots.

    ○ **Correction:** God used the unique personalities, backgrounds, and writing styles of the human authors while perfectly guiding what they wrote.

- **Misunderstanding:** The Bible is a magical rulebook that guarantees a perfect life if we follow it.

    ○ **Correction:** The Bible is primarily a story about God rescuing broken people through Jesus, not a formula for an easy, pain-free life.

- **Misunderstanding:** Some parts of the Bible are from God, and other parts are just human opinions.

    ○ **Correction:** All of Scripture is breathed out by God. We cannot pick and choose the parts we like while discarding the parts that challenge or offend us.

How to Answer Follow-Up Questions If they ask: "How do we know the Bible is actually true?" **Say:** "We can trust the Bible because Jesus trusted it. Jesus treated the Old Testament as the absolute Word of God, and He promised that the Holy Spirit would guide His disciples to write the New Testament."

If they ask: "Why doesn't the Bible talk about modern things like smartphones?" **Say:** "The Bible doesn't mention every specific invention, but it gives us timeless wisdom about how to use our time, how to treat others, and how to guard our hearts, which perfectly applies to how we use smartphones today."

If they ask: "What if I read the Bible and don't understand it?" **Say:** "That happens to adults, too! The Bible is deep enough for scholars to study for a lifetime, but simple enough for a child to understand its main point. When you're confused, that's exactly why we have parents, pastors, and the Holy Spirit to help explain it."

Extra Bible Anchors for Parents Psalm 119:89; Isaiah 55:10–11; Hebrews 4:12 2 Timothy 3:16–17 , "All Scripture is inspired by God and is profitable for teaching, for rebuking, for correcting, for training in righteousness, so that the man of God may be complete, equipped for every good work." (CSB)

Teach-It-Back Prompt Sometime tomorrow, casually ask: 'If a friend asked you who wrote the Bible, how would you explain that both God and humans wrote it?'

MEMORY (One-Liner + Catechism Q/A)

One-Liner: The Bible is God's true and perfect Word.

Optional Q&A: Q: Who wrote the Bible? A: God the Holy Spirit guided human authors to write exactly what He wanted.

Notes:

WEEK 3: HOW TO READ THE BIBLE

BLOCK 1: KID PAGE (Big Idea + Anchor Verse)

Big Idea: The Bible is a library of different books that tell one big story about Jesus. To understand what God is saying, we can't just pick one verse and ignore the rest; we have to look at the "context", who wrote it, who they wrote to, and what the verses around it say. Reading the Bible wisely means paying attention to the whole picture.

Anchor Verse: Psalm 119:18

In kid words: God, please open my eyes so I can see the amazing and wonderful truths in Your teachings.

Key Words:

- **Context:** The parts of the story that happen before and after a specific verse. (Context helps us understand what is actually happening).

- **Genre:** The type of writing. (The Bible has history, poetry, letters, and songs, we read them differently).

More Bible places to look: Nehemiah 8:8; Psalm 1:2; Luke 24:27; Acts 8:30–31; Acts 17:11; 2 Timothy 2:15

BLOCK 2: STORY PAGE (Real Life Scenario)

Story Title: The Science Class Confusion

Setting: Marcus came home from school and dropped his backpack on the floor with a heavy thud, looking more worried than usual.

Problem: In science class, his teacher had explained how rain is formed by evaporation and clouds, but Marcus remembered a verse that said God sends the rain. He felt like he had to choose between what he learned in his textbook and what he read in his Bible. He wondered, "Is the Bible wrong, or is my science teacher wrong?"

Choice moment: *I could just push the confusion away and pretend I don't care,* Marcus thought, *or I could be brave and ask my dad how these two things fit together.*

Small resolution: Marcus asked his dad, "Does God send the rain, or does the water cycle make it?" His dad smiled and opened the Bible. "It's both, Marcus. The Bible isn't a science textbook explaining *how* water molecules work; it's a book telling us *Who* is in charge of it all. Science explains the tool; the Bible reveals the Artist using it."

Quick takeaway: We read the Bible to learn the truth about *Who* God is, not to answer every science question about *how* the world works.

BLOCK 3: TALK-IT-OUT (Discussion + Coaching)

1. **Understanding:** Imagine you only saw one tiny corner of a puzzle piece. Would you know what the whole picture was? How is that like reading a Bible verse without context?

2. **Connection to life:** Have you ever been confused by something you read in the Bible because it sounded strange or scary?

3. **Application:** Is there a Bible story or verse that has always confused you? Let's write it down today and try to find the answer together.

If your kid says: "The Bible is too hard to understand." **Try:** "It can be tricky! Even adults find it hard sometimes. That's why we don't have to read it alone. We have the Holy Spirit to help us, and we have each other to talk about it."

If your kid says: "Why doesn't the Bible just say things plainly?" **Try:** "God chose to give us a beautiful book full of stories, songs, and letters instead of just a list of instructions. Stories help us know Him as a person, not just a rule-maker."

BLOCK 4: PRACTICE (One Habit This Week)

Habit: The "Who, What, Where" Check.

When we'll do it: When we read a Bible story this week, we will pause and ask: "Who is writing this?", "Who are they writing to?", and "What happened right before this?"

What to watch for: Your child realizing that Bible verses belong to real stories involving real people, rather than just being magic quotes.

Prayer: Father, thank You for Your Word. Give us wisdom to read it carefully, to understand the full story, and to see Jesus on every page. Amen.

BLOCK 5: PARENT NOTES (The Secret Weapon)

The Doctrine, Precisely This week focuses on *hermeneutics*, which is the fancy word for "how to interpret the Bible." A common error in family discipleship is treating the Bible like a fortune cookie, picking a random verse, ignoring the context, and applying it immediately to our situation. To read the Bible faithfully, we must respect the author's intent.

We teach our kids to consider the *Genre* (is this a poem, a law, or a letter?), the *Context* (what did this mean to the original audience?), and the *Christ-Connection* (how does this point to Jesus?). When we skip these steps, we risk making the Bible say things God never intended.

Why It Matters

- **It protects us from mistakes:** Many false ideas come from taking a single verse out of context (e.g., "I can do all things through Christ" usually gets applied to sports, but Paul was writing about enduring starvation and prison).

- **It respects God's method:** God chose to communicate through history and literature. Honoring the literary style is a way of honoring God.

- **It reduces confusion:** When kids understand that a Psalm is a poem expressing emotion (and not a promise that God will crush our enemies' teeth), they are less likely to be confused by "scary" verses.

Common Misunderstandings to Avoid

- **Misunderstanding:** "What does this verse mean to me?" is the first question we should ask.

  - **Correction:** The first question is always, "What did this mean to the original author and audience?" Only *after* we answer that can we ask how it applies to us.

- **Misunderstanding:** Every verse in the Bible is a promise for me personally.

  - **Correction:** Some verses are historical records of what happened, or specific promises to specific people (like Israel). All Scripture is *for* us, but not all Scripture is *about* us.

- **Misunderstanding:** You have to be an expert to understand the Bible.

  - **Correction:** The main things are the plain things. While context helps, the central message of the Gospel is clear enough for a child to grasp.

How to Answer Follow-Up Questions If they ask: "Why are there so many different translations of the Bible?" **Say:** "The Bible was originally written in Hebrew and Greek. Different translations are just teams of scholars trying their best to turn those ancient languages into English we can understand today."

If they ask: "Why does the Old Testament seem so different from the New Testament?" **Say:** "It's the same story, just different chapters. The Old Testament is like the 'shadow' showing us that we need a Rescuer. The New Testament is the 'reality' showing us that the Rescuer is Jesus."

If they ask: "What if I see a verse that seems to contradict science?" **Say:** "The Bible and the world were both made by the same God, so they can't truly disagree. Usually, if there is a conflict, it means we are either misunderstanding the science or misunderstanding what the Bible is trying to teach us."

Extra Bible Anchors for Parents Luke 24:44–45; Acts 8:30–35; 2 Peter 3:15–16 Psalm 119:130 , "The revelation of your words brings light and gives understanding to the inexperienced." (CSB)

Teach-It-Back Prompt Challenge your child to explain "Context" using a puzzle analogy: "If you hold up just one puzzle piece, can you tell what the whole picture is? No! You need the pieces around it. That's context."

MEMORY (One-Liner + Catechism Q/A)

One-Liner: Context means reading the whole story, not just one verse.

Optional Q&A: Q: How do we read the Bible wisely? A: We look at who wrote it, who they wrote to, and how it points to Jesus.

Notes:

WEEK 4: TRUTH & FAITH

BLOCK 1: KID PAGE (Big Idea + Anchor Verse)

Big Idea: Faith is not wishing for things to happen or pretending that everything is okay when it isn't. Faith is trusting that God is telling the truth about who He is and what He has done. Even when we are scared or have questions, we can have faith because we know God keeps His promises.

Anchor Verse: Hebrews 11:1

In kid words: Faith is acting like God is telling the truth, even before we see how the story ends.

Key Words:

- **Faith:** Trusting in God and His Word, even when we can't see Him with our eyes.

- **Truth:** What is real and right, exactly as God sees it.

More Bible places to look: Proverbs 3:5–6; Mark 9:24; John 14:1; John 14:6; Romans 10:17; Ephesians 2:8–9

BLOCK 2: STORY PAGE (Real Life Scenario)

Story Title: The Big Test Panic

Setting: Chloe sat at her desk, staring at her math textbook. The numbers seemed to be swimming on the page.

Problem: She had a massive test tomorrow, and math was her hardest subject. Her stomach felt like it was tied in knots. She closed her eyes tight and prayed, "God, please, please, just let me get an A. I promise I'll be good if You just give me an A." She opened her eyes, but she didn't feel any better. She felt like she was just making a wish, not really praying.

Choice moment: *I can keep panicking and treating God like a genie,* Chloe thought, *or I can ask Him for peace and actually study hard.*

Small resolution: Chloe took a deep breath. She prayed again, but this time she said, "God, I'm scared. I don't know if I'll get an A, but I know You are with me. Please help me think clearly." She didn't magically know all the answers, but she felt steady enough to open her book and start studying, trusting God to handle the results.

Quick takeaway: Faith isn't a magic trick to get what we want; it's trusting that God is with us even when things are hard.

BLOCK 3: TALK-IT-OUT (Discussion + Coaching)

1. **Understanding:** In the story, Chloe realized she was treating God like a genie. How is having faith different than just making a wish?

2. **Connection to life:** Have you ever prayed for something really hard, like Chloe, and felt scared that God wouldn't do it?

3. **Application:** What is one true promise from the Bible that you can trust this week? (Examples: "I am with you," "I will forgive you," or "I hear your prayers").

If your kid says: "I tried having faith, but God didn't give me what I asked for." **Try:** "That is really hard. But faith isn't about getting exactly what we want; it's about trusting that God knows what is best for us, even when His answer is 'no' or 'wait.'"

If your kid says: "I don't feel like I have enough faith." **Try:** "The good news is that it's not the *size* of your faith that matters; it's *Who* your faith is in. Even a tiny amount of faith in a big, strong God is enough."

BLOCK 4: PRACTICE (One Habit This Week)

Habit: The "I Trust You" Prayer.

When we'll do it: Before we do something difficult this week (like a test, a chore, or a hard conversation), we will stop and say, "God, I don't know how this will go, but I trust You."

What to watch for: A shift from asking for magic results to asking for God's presence and help.

Prayer: Lord, we believe; help our unbelief! Thank You that You are the Way, the Truth, and the Life, and that we can trust You completely. Amen.

BLOCK 5: PARENT NOTES (The Secret Weapon)

The Doctrine, Precisely In our culture, "faith" is often redefined as positive thinking. Biblical faith is radically different. It is *fiducia*, which means leaning your whole weight on something. It isn't a blind leap into the dark; it is a confident step into the light, based on the evidence of who God is and what He has done.

We want our kids to understand that faith is an instrument. It is the hand that reaches out to receive God's grace. The power of faith does not come from how hard we squeeze our eyes shut and believe; the power comes from the Object of our faith: Christ Himself.

Why It Matters

- **It anchors emotions:** Kids often feel like their faith is "gone" if they don't *feel* happy or spiritual. Teaching them that faith is a choice to trust God's truth, regardless of feelings, creates stability.

- **It clarifies salvation:** We are saved by grace *through faith*. Understanding that faith is receiving (not earning) is the key to understanding the Gospel.

- **It combats skepticism:** Faith is not the opposite of knowledge. We have good reasons to believe. Faith is simply acting on that knowledge.

Common Misunderstandings to Avoid

- **Misunderstanding:** Faith means checking your brain at the door.

  - **Correction:** God commands us to love Him with our *minds*. Faith acts on the best evidence we have, God's Word.

- **Misunderstanding:** If I have enough faith, nothing bad will happen to me.

  - **Correction:** Many heroes of the faith (like in Hebrews 11) suffered greatly. Faith doesn't prevent storms; it grounds us *in* the storm.

- **Misunderstanding:** Faith is a feeling.

  - **Correction:** Faith is loyalty and trust. You can have faith in your parents even when you are angry with them. You can have faith in God even when you are sad.

How to Answer Follow-Up Questions If they ask: "What if I have doubts?" **Say:** "Doubts are like questions that are looking for answers. It's okay to have them! Bring your doubts to God and to us. We can look for the answers together."

If they ask: "Does God lie?" **Say:** "Never. The Bible says it is impossible for God to lie. That is why we can trust Him more than we trust anyone else, even more than we trust our own feelings."

If they ask: "Why can't I see God if I'm supposed to trust Him?" **Say:** "We trust lots of things we can't see, like the wind or gravity, because we see what they *do*. We see what God does in the world and in our hearts, so we know He is there."

Extra Bible Anchors for Parents Numbers 23:19; Psalm 33:4; Romans 4:20–21 Hebrews 11:6 , "Now without faith it is impossible to please God, since the one who draws near to him must believe that he exists and that he rewards those who seek him." (CSB)

Teach-It-Back Prompt Ask your child to imagine a chair. Ask them, "Do you believe this chair holds people up?" (Yes). "Do you have faith in it right now?" (No, not until you sit in it). Faith is sitting in the chair.

MEMORY (One-Liner + Catechism Q/A)

One-Liner: Faith is trusting that God tells the truth.

Optional Q&A: Q: What is faith? A: Faith is trusting God and His Word more than our own feelings.

Notes:

BLOCK 1: KID PAGE (Big Idea + Anchor Verse)

Big Idea: Prayer is simply talking to God and listening to Him. We don't need fancy words or a special voice; we just need to be honest. Because of Jesus, we can talk to the Creator of the universe like a child talks to a loving father, anytime and anywhere.

Anchor Verse: Philippians 4:6–7

In kid words: Don't worry about anything; instead, pray about everything. Tell God what you need and thank Him for all He has done.

Key Words:

- **Prayer:** Talking to God and listening to Him.

- **Petition:** Asking God for what we need.

- **Thanksgiving:** Thanking God for who He is and what He has done.

More Bible places to look: Psalm 62:8; Matthew 6:5–13; Luke 18:1; Romans 8:26; 1 Thessalonians 5:17; 1 Peter 5:7

BLOCK 2: STORY PAGE (Real Life Scenario)

Story Title: The Scary Shadow

Setting: Liam lay in his bed, staring at the closet door. It was mostly shut, but the streetlight outside made a weird, long shadow that looked like a monster's hand.

Problem: His heart started beating fast. He pulled the covers up to his nose. He tried to remember a prayer he learned at church, but he got the words mixed up. He thought, "If I don't say the prayer exactly right, God won't hear me, and I'll be unsafe."

Choice moment: *I can hide under the blankets and worry about using fancy words,* Liam thought, *or I can just talk to God like He's right here in the room.*

Small resolution: Liam whispered, "God, I'm really scared of that shadow. Please help me be brave so I can sleep." He didn't feel a zap of lightning, but he felt a little quieter inside. He reached over, turned on his nightlight, and saw the shadow was just his bathrobe.

Quick takeaway: We don't need perfect words to talk to God; we just need to tell Him the truth about how we feel.

BLOCK 3: TALK-IT-OUT (Discussion + Coaching)

1. **Understanding:** If God already knows exactly what we need before we ask, why does He still want us to pray?

2. **Connection to life:** Is there a time of day (like bedtime or before a test) when you talk to God the most?

3. **Application:** What is one thing you are worried about right now that you can talk to God about?

If your kid says: "I don't know what to say when I pray." **Try:** "That happens to everyone! You can use a simple pattern: 'Thank You, God, for...' 'Sorry, God, for...' and 'Please, God, help...'"

If your kid says: "It feels weird talking to someone I can't see." **Try:** "It definitely feels different at first. Think of it like talking on the phone to Grandma. You can't see her, but you know she's listening and she loves you."

BLOCK 4: PRACTICE (One Habit This Week)

Habit: The "Breath Prayer."

When we'll do it: When we feel scared, angry, or happy this week, we will say a super short prayer in one breath. (Example: "Lord, help me." or "Thank You, Jesus.")

What to watch for: Your child realizing that prayer doesn't have to be long or formal; it can happen in the middle of playing or school.

Prayer: Our Father, thank You that You always listen to us. Teach us to pray with honest hearts and to trust that You love to hear our voices. Amen.

BLOCK 5: PARENT NOTES (The Secret Weapon)

The Doctrine, Precisely Prayer is the personal communication between a believer and God. It is an act of worship and dependence. Theologically, prayer is grounded in our adoption: because we are children of God through Christ, we have access to the Father. We do not pray to alert God to information He doesn't know; we pray to align our hearts with His will and to deepen our relationship with Him.

We teach our kids that prayer includes *Adoration* (praising God), *Confession* (admitting sin), *Thanksgiving* (gratitude), and *Supplication* (asking for needs), often remembered by the acronym ACTS. But primarily, we want them to know that God is a Person, not a vending machine.

Why It Matters

- **It kills pride:** Prayer reminds us that we are not in control and that we need help. This is the root of humility.

- **It builds relationship:** You cannot be close to someone you never speak to. Prayer is the lifeline of our relationship with God.

- **It relieves anxiety:** Teaching kids to offload their worries onto God ("casting all your cares on Him") is one of the most practical mental health tools we can give them.

Common Misunderstandings to Avoid

- **Misunderstanding:** Prayer is a magic spell; if I say the right words, I get what I want.

  - **Correction:** God is a Father who loves us, not a genie who obeys us. He gives us what is good, not always exactly what we ask for.

- **Misunderstanding:** I have to be in a special place or position to pray.

  - **Correction:** Posture (kneeling, closing eyes) helps us focus, but you can pray walking, driving, or lying in bed. God listens to the heart, not the knees.

- **Misunderstanding:** God only listens to adults or pastors.

  - **Correction:** God loves the prayers of children. In fact, Jesus told the adults to become more like children!

How to Answer Follow-Up Questions If they ask: "Why didn't God answer my prayer?" **Say:** "God always answers. Sometimes He says 'Yes,' sometimes He says 'No' because He sees danger we don't see, and sometimes He says 'Wait' to help us grow patience."

If they ask: "Does prayer change God's mind?" **Say:** "That's a deep question! The Bible tells us God is in charge of everything, but it also tells us our prayers matter and make things happen. We pray because God invites us to be part of what He is doing."

If they ask: "Why do we say 'Amen'?" **Say:** "Amen is a Hebrew word that means 'Truth' or 'Let it be so.' It's like signing your name at the end of a letter. It means, 'I really mean this.'"

Extra Bible Anchors for Parents Psalm 145:18; Matthew 7:7–11; 1 John 5:14 1 Thessalonians 5:16–18 , "Rejoice always, pray constantly, give thanks in everything; for this is God's will for you in Christ Jesus." (CSB)

Teach-It-Back Prompt Hold up your hand and teach your child the "Five Finger Prayer":

1. Thumb (closest to you): Pray for family.

2. Pointer: Pray for teachers/leaders.

3. Tall finger: Pray for those in charge/government.

4. Ring finger (weakest): Pray for the sick/poor.

5. Pinky: Pray for yourself.

MEMORY (One-Liner + Catechism Q/A)

One-Liner: Prayer is talking to God with an honest heart.

Optional Q&A: Q: How do we pray? A: We pray to the Father, through the Son, with the help of the Holy Spirit.

Notes:

WEEK 6: REVIEW: BUILD YOUR TOOLBOX

BLOCK 1: KID PAGE (Big Idea + Anchor Verse)

Big Idea: We have learned five big tools for our faith: Theology, the Bible, Context, Faith, and Prayer. Just like a builder needs to know how to use a hammer and a saw, we need to practice using these truths so we can build a strong life with God. Reviewing what we learned helps us keep these tools sharp and ready to use.

Anchor Verse: Psalm 119:11

In kid words: I have stored up your word in my heart so that I might not sin against you.

Key Words:

- **Review:** Looking back at what we learned to make sure we remember it.

- **Disciple:** A learner and follower of Jesus who practices what He teaches.

More Bible places to look: Deuteronomy 6:6–9; Joshua 1:8; Psalm 1:1–3; Luke 6:47–48; Colossians 3:16; James 1:22–25

BLOCK 2: STORY PAGE (Real Life Scenario)

Story Title: The Family Meeting Grump

Setting: Jackson was sitting on the living room rug while his dad opened the Bible for their family devotion time.

Problem: Jackson let out a loud, dramatic groan and flopped backward. "Do we *have* to do this again?" he complained. "We did it last week! I already know all this stuff." He felt annoyed that he had to pause his video game to talk about things he thought he already understood perfectly.

Choice moment: *I can keep complaining and make everyone miserable,* Jackson thought, *or I can sit up and actually listen, just to see if there is something I missed.*

Small resolution: His dad didn't get angry but simply said, "Jackson, pro athletes still practice the basics every single day. We do this because we forget fast." Jackson sighed, sat up crisscross-applesauce, and decided to actually listen. Surprisingly, when they talked about prayer, he realized he had forgotten the part about "listening," not just asking.

Quick takeaway: We practice our faith over and over not because we are dumb, but because our hearts are prone to forget.

BLOCK 3: TALK-IT-OUT (Discussion + Coaching)

1. **Understanding:** Why do you think athletes (or musicians) practice the same simple moves over and over again? How is that like our faith?

2. **Connection to life:** Which of the five topics we learned so far (Theology, Bible, Reading Context, Faith, Prayer) was your favorite? Which one was the hardest?

3. **Application:** Let's flip back through the book together. Can you find the 'Big Idea' for Week 1 and read it to me?

If your kid says: "This is boring." **Try:** "I get that. Sometimes repetition feels boring. But think about brushing your teeth, it's not exciting, but if you stop doing it, your teeth rot. Reviewing truth keeps our hearts healthy."

If your kid says: "I already know this." **Try:** "Knowing the *answer* is different than living the *truth*. You might know that an apple is healthy, but that doesn't help you unless you actually eat it."

BLOCK 4: PRACTICE (One Habit This Week)

Habit: The "Toolbox Check."

When we'll do it: At dinner one night, we will go around the table and ask: "What is one 'tool' from God (like prayer or Bible reading) that you used this week?"

What to watch for: Your child recognizing that theology isn't just for this book, but for their actual life at school and home.

Prayer: Lord, thank You for the truth You have given us. Please write these lessons on our hearts so we don't forget them, and help us to use these tools to love You more every day. Amen.

BLOCK 5: PARENT NOTES (The Secret Weapon)

The Doctrine, Precisely This week is about *catechesis* (instruction) and *sanctification*. We are solidifying the foundation. The goal of review is not merely information retention (passing a test) but spiritual formation (shaping the heart). We are establishing a "liturgy" of remembrance. The Bible constantly commands God's people to "remember" because the default mode of the human heart is to drift, forget, and idolize.

Review weeks allow you to gauge where the concepts landed. Did the definition of "faith" stick? Is "context" still a fuzzy concept? Use this week to patch cracks in the foundation before adding more weight in Part 2.

Why It Matters

- **It fights spiritual amnesia:** Israel frequently forgot God's miracles in the wilderness and immediately fell into sin. Regular review is our defense against forgetting God's goodness.

- **It values depth over width:** It is better for a child to deeply understand and apply five truths than to vaguely remember fifty.

- **It models humility:** By reviewing, parents show that they are also learners who need reminders, not just experts dispensing new facts.

Common Misunderstandings to Avoid

- **Misunderstanding:** If my kid can repeat the definition, they have "learned" it.

  - **Correction:** Intellectual assent is the first step, not the final destination. Look for signs of *application* (e.g., stopping to pray when scared).

- **Misunderstanding:** Review weeks are "off weeks" where we don't do anything.

  - **Correction:** Review weeks are "work weeks." They are where the cement dries. Treat them with the same importance as new content weeks.

How to Answer Follow-Up Questions If they ask: "Why does the Bible say the same things over and over?" **Say:** "Because God knows how we are built. He knows we get distracted easily, so He repeats the most important things, like 'do not fear', so we finally hear them."

If they ask: "Can we skip this week?" **Say:** "We could, but then we might miss something big. Think of it like tightening the screws on a bike. You check them to make sure the wheels don't fall off later!"

Extra Bible Anchors for Parents Deuteronomy 4:9; Psalm 77:11; 2 Peter 1:12–13 Psalm 119:11 , "I have stored up your word in my heart so that I might not sin against you." (CSB)

Teach-It-Back Prompt Play "Stump the Parent." Let your child open the book to one of the previous weeks (Theology, Bible, Context, Faith, Prayer) and quiz *you* on what it means. If you get it wrong, they get a point!

<u>MEMORY (One-Liner + Catechism Q/A)</u>

One-Liner: We practice what we know so we don't forget it.

Optional Q&A: Q: Why do we review God's truth? A: We review because we are prone to forget, and we want God's truth to stay in our hearts.

<u>Notes:</u>

WEEK 7: LIFE SKILL: HOW TO ASK GOOD QUESTIONS

BLOCK 1: KID PAGE (Big Idea + Anchor Verse)

Big Idea: Asking questions isn't a sign of weakness; it is the key that unlocks wisdom. It shows you are growing. God gave us minds to think and be curious. When we don't understand something about God, the Bible, or the world, the best thing we can do is ask a humble question to someone we trust.

Anchor Verse: Proverbs 2:3–5

In kid words: Cry out for wisdom and ask for understanding. Look for it like hidden treasure, and you will find the knowledge of God.

Key Words:

- **Humility:** Admitting that we don't know everything and need help.

- **Curiosity:** The desire to learn more about who God is and what He has made.

More Bible places to look: 1 Kings 3:9; Matthew 7:7; Luke 2:46; Acts 17:11; James 1:5

BLOCK 2: STORY PAGE (Real Life Scenario)

Story Title: The Red Pen Mark

Setting: Mia sat at her desk in the middle of a quiet classroom. Her teacher, Mr. Harrison, was handing back graded quizzes.

Problem: When Mr. Harrison dropped Mia's paper on her desk, she saw a big red "X" next to an answer she thought she knew perfectly. Her cheeks turned hot and red. She felt embarrassed and angry. She wanted to crumple the paper up and hide it, or maybe argue that the teacher was wrong.

Choice moment: *I can hide the paper so no one sees I'm not perfect,* Mia thought, *or I can be brave, go up to the desk, and ask, 'Can you help me understand this?'*

Small resolution: Mia took a shaky breath and walked up to Mr. Harrison's desk. "I thought I had this right," she whispered. "Can you explain it?" Mr. Harrison smiled kindly. "I'm so glad you asked, Mia. Look here." He showed her a step she missed. Mia still didn't like the red X, but she wasn't scared of the mistake anymore because she learned from it.

Quick takeaway: Mistakes are just opportunities to ask good questions and get smarter.

BLOCK 3: TALK-IT-OUT (Discussion + Coaching)

1. **Understanding:** What is the biggest fear you have about asking a question? (That people will laugh? That you'll look silly?)

2. **Connection to life:** Have you ever pretended to know the answer when you really didn't? How did that feel?

3. **Application:** Who are three people in your life that you trust to give you true answers when you have a hard question?

If your kid says: "I'm afraid people will laugh at me if I ask." **Try:** "That is a very real fear. But actually, usually when you ask a question, three other people in the room are thinking, 'Oh, thank goodness someone asked that!'"

If your kid says: "I don't agree with what the teacher/pastor said." **Try:** "It is okay to disagree! The best way to handle that is to ask a respectful question like, 'I heard you say X, but the Bible seems to say Y. Can you help me understand?'"

BLOCK 4: PRACTICE (One Habit This Week)

Habit: The "One Why" Day.

When we'll do it: On Saturday (or a day off), try to ask "Why?" about three things you see in nature or the Bible. (e.g., 'I wonder why God made the sky blue?' or 'I wonder why Jesus said that?')

What to watch for: Your child moving from just accepting things to actively wondering about God's design.

Prayer: God of all wisdom, thank You for giving us minds to think. Help us to be humble enough to ask for help and curious enough to seek Your truth. Amen.

BLOCK 5: PARENT NOTES (The Secret Weapon)

The Doctrine, Precisely This week focuses on the virtue of *intellectual humility*. In a discipleship context, we want to shift the paradigm from "faith means never questioning" to "faith means seeking understanding." This is the classic motto *faith seeking understanding* (fides quaerens intellectum).

We are teaching our kids that God is not threatened by their curiosity. However, the *posture* of the question matters. There is a difference between the questions of a skeptic (asking to trap or mock) and the questions of a disciple (asking to learn and obey). We want to model and reward the latter.

Why It Matters

- **It builds resilience:** A child who is taught to suppress questions will eventually encounter a question they can't suppress, and their faith may crumble. A child taught to *wrestle* with questions builds a faith that can survive doubts.

- **It encourages wisdom:** The book of Proverbs is essentially a training manual on asking for and receiving wisdom.

- **It deepens relationship:** We want our kids to come to *us* with their hardest questions about sex, culture, and pain, not to Reddit or their peers. How we handle the small questions now sets the precedent for the big questions later.

Common Misunderstandings to Avoid

- **Misunderstanding:** Asking questions is a sign of weak faith.

    ◦ **Correction:** Asking questions is often a sign of a living faith that wants to grow. Jesus Himself asked questions!

- **Misunderstanding:** As a parent, I need to have all the answers immediately.

    ◦ **Correction:** It is powerful to say, "I don't know the answer to that. That is a great question. Let's research it together."

How to Answer Follow-Up Questions If they ask: "Are there any bad questions?" **Say:** "There aren't really 'bad' questions, but there are bad *attitudes*. Asking 'Why do I have to do this?' with a whine is different than asking 'Can you explain why this rule matters?' with a calm voice."

If they ask: "What if we ask and still don't find the answer?" **Say:** "That happens sometimes. God has told us everything we *need* to know, but not everything there is to know. We trust Him with the secrets He hasn't shared yet."

Extra Bible Anchors for Parents Proverbs 18:15; Matthew 7:7–8; Luke 2:46–47 Proverbs 2:6 , "For the Lord gives wisdom; from his mouth come knowledge and understanding." (CSB)

Teach-It-Back Prompt Practice the "I Don't Know" dance. Ask your child a super hard question (like 'Why did God allow mosquitoes?' or 'When is Jesus coming back?'). Teach them to confidently shrug and say, "I don't know, but I can find out!"

MEMORY (One-Liner + Catechism Q/A)

One-Liner: Asking good questions helps us grow in wisdom.

Optional Q&A: Q: What should we do if we don't understand something? A: We should ask God for wisdom and ask others for help.

Notes:

WEEK 8: LIFE SKILL: HOW TO DISAGREE WITH KINDNESS

BLOCK 1: KID PAGE (Big Idea + Anchor Verse)

Big Idea: Because we live in a world where people believe different things, we will often disagree with others. God calls us to speak the truth (not hiding what we believe) but to do it with love (not being mean or rude). We can disagree with someone's ideas while still treating them with respect as a person made by God.

Anchor Verse: Ephesians 4:15

In kid words: We should speak the truth in love so that we can grow up to be like Jesus.

Key Words:

- **Gentleness:** Power under control. (Think of a strong hand holding a tiny bird gently so it doesn't get hurt).

- **Respect:** Treating someone like they are valuable, even if they are wrong.

More Bible places to look: Proverbs 15:1; Romans 12:18; 1 Corinthians 13:4–5; Colossians 4:6; 2 Timothy 2:24–25; 1 Peter 3:15

BLOCK 2: STORY PAGE (Real Life Scenario)

Story Title: The Group Chat Heat

Setting: Caleb was playing his favorite video game online with a group of friends from school. They were using a group chat to talk while they played.

Problem: One of his friends, Ty, typed something really mean about a kid at their school who wasn't playing. Then Ty added, "If you don't agree, you're an idiot too." Caleb felt his face get hot. He knew Ty was wrong to bully the kid, but he was scared to say anything. He wanted to type back a mean insult to shut Ty up.

Choice moment: *I can roast Ty with a mean joke and make everyone laugh at him,* Caleb thought, *or I can be brave enough to say the truth without being mean.*

Small resolution: Caleb paused and typed, "Ty, you're my friend, but that's not cool. We shouldn't talk about people like that." Ty replied with a "Whatever," and the chat got quiet for a minute. Caleb didn't "win" the fight, and Ty didn't apologize right away, but Caleb felt good knowing he stood up for the truth without becoming a bully himself.

Quick takeaway: Standing for truth doesn't mean we have to start a war; we can be firm and kind at the same time.

BLOCK 3: TALK-IT-OUT (Discussion + Coaching)

1. **Understanding:** Why is it so much easier to be mean to someone when you can't see their face (like online or in a video game)?

2. **Connection to life:** Have you ever seen someone get really angry just because someone disagreed with them? How did that make them look?

3. **Application:** Is there anyone you are mad at right now because you disagree? How can you show them kindness this week?

If your kid says: "But if I'm nice, they'll think I agree with them!" **Try:** "That's a tricky balance. But you can say, 'I definitely don't agree with that, but I'm not going to fight with you about it.' That shows you are strong, not weak."

If your kid says: "They started it!" **Try:** "I know they did. But as followers of Jesus, we don't let other people's bad behavior control our behavior. We answer to God, not to them."

BLOCK 4: PRACTICE (One Habit This Week)

Habit: The "Pause Button."

When we'll do it: When we feel our face getting hot or our voice getting loud during an argument (with a sibling or friend), we will physically press an imaginary "Pause Button" on our chest and take three seconds to pray, 'Help me be kind,' before speaking.

What to watch for: A decrease in "snapping back" and an increase in self-control.

Prayer: Lord Jesus, You were always full of grace and truth. Please help my words to be kind, even when I disagree, and help me to love people more than I love winning an argument. Amen.

BLOCK 5: PARENT NOTES (The Secret Weapon)

The Doctrine, Precisely This week tackles the crucial balance of *grace and truth*. Culturally, we are drifting into two extremes: (1) aggressive tribalism, where disagreement equals hatred, or (2) relativistic niceness, where disagreement is seen as intolerance. We want to equip our kids with a "third way", the way of Christ.

We are teaching *convictional civility*. This means holding firm biblical convictions (not compromising truth) while maintaining a posture of civility and love toward those who oppose us (not compromising grace). This is grounded in the doctrine of the *Imago Dei* (Image of God), our opponent is a bearer of God's image and deserves dignity, even if their ideas are dangerous or wrong.

Why It Matters

- **It distinguishes us:** The world shouts and cancels. Christians who can disagree with gentleness shine like stars in a dark sky (Philippians 2:15).

- **It preserves relationships:** Winning an argument is rarely worth losing a friend or a brother. Kindness keeps the bridge open for the Gospel.

- **It reflects God's heart:** God is kind to the ungrateful and the wicked (Luke 6:35). When we are kind to those we disagree with, we act like our Father.

Common Misunderstandings to Avoid

- **Misunderstanding:** "Speaking the truth in love" means just being nice and never saying they are wrong.

  - **Correction:** Love sometimes requires saying hard things. A doctor who doesn't tell you about your illness isn't loving. But the *tone* matters.

- **Misunderstanding:** If I am right, I have the right to be angry.

  - **Correction:** James 1:20 tells us that human anger does not produce the righteousness of God. Truth spoken in anger is often rejected because of the anger, not the truth.

How to Answer Follow-Up Questions If they ask: "What if they are saying something really bad about God?" **Say:** "It hurts to hear that. But defending God doesn't mean acting like the devil. We defend God best by showing them what God is like, patient and truthful."

If they ask: "What if they just keep being mean to me?" **Say:** "Then you can stop the conversation. Being kind doesn't mean you have to stay there and be a punching bag. You can walk away."

Extra Bible Anchors for Parents Proverbs 15:1; Luke 6:27–28; Titus 3:2 1 Peter 3:15 , "But in your hearts regard Christ the Lord as holy, ready at any time to give a defense to anyone who asks you for a reason for the hope that is in you." (CSB)

Teach-It-Back Prompt Roleplay: Start small. Pretend to argue about something silly, like 'Pineapple belongs on pizza.' Then try a harder one, like 'Cheating is okay if you don't get caught.' Practice disagreeing without rolling eyes or yelling.

MEMORY (One-Liner + Catechism Q/A)

One-Liner: We speak the truth with love, not with anger.

Optional Q&A: Q: How should we treat people who disagree with us? A: We should treat them with respect and gentleness.

Notes:

WEEK 9: LIFE SKILL: BUILDING A FAMILY HABIT

BLOCK 1: KID PAGE (Big Idea + Anchor Verse)

Big Idea: Habits are things we do over and over until we don't even have to think about them, like brushing our teeth or tying our shoes. Spiritual habits (like praying, reading the Bible, or going to church) are exercises for our hearts. They train us to love God more, even on days when we don't "feel" like it.

Anchor Verse: 1 Timothy 4:7–8

In kid words: Train yourself for a godly life. Exercise is good for your body, but training your heart for God is even better because it lasts forever.

Key Words:

- **Habit:** Something we practice regularly so it becomes part of our normal life.

- **Discipline:** Training our bodies and minds to do what is right, even when it is hard.

More Bible places to look: Psalm 1:2; Daniel 6:10; Luke 4:16; Acts 2:42; Hebrews 10:24–25; Hebrews 12:11

BLOCK 2: STORY PAGE (Real Life Scenario)

Story Title: The Glowing Screen   **Setting:** It was 9:30 PM. The house was dark and quiet. Ava was supposed to be asleep, but she was under her covers with her tablet.

Problem: Ava knew the family rule: "No screens in the bedroom at night." But she really wanted to finish watching a video. It started as "just one minute," but now it had been twenty minutes. She knew she was building a bad habit of sneaking and hiding, and it made her stomach feel twisted with guilt.

Choice moment: *I can listen to the voice that says 'just five more minutes,'* Ava thought, *or I can choose to stop right now, even though I really want to see the end.*

Small resolution: Ava paused the video. The fun wasn't worth the guilt. She crept out of bed, walked down the hallway, and plugged the tablet into the charger in the kitchen. The next morning, she told her mom, "I had the tablet in my room last night, but I put it back." Her mom was serious but glad. "Thank you for being honest, Ava. Let's work on keeping that temptation out of your room tonight."

Quick takeaway: Good habits (like honesty and sleep!) protect us, while secret habits can trap us.

BLOCK 3: TALK-IT-OUT (Discussion + Coaching)

1. **Understanding:** Why do you think athletes train and practice even when they are tired? How is that like being a Christian?

2. **Connection to life:** What is one "bad habit" you have (like biting nails, interrupting, or sneaking screens)? What is one "good habit" you have?

3. **Application:** What is one small spiritual habit we could start as a family this week? (Examples: Prayer at breakfast, reading one verse before bed, no screens after dinner).

If your kid says: "Habits are boring. I want my faith to be exciting!" **Try:** "I love excitement too! But think about a musician. They play boring scales for hours so that when the concert comes, they can play an amazing solo. Our habits get us ready for the big moments."

If your kid says: "I try to start habits but I always quit." **Try:** "That is normal. The key isn't being perfect; it's starting again. If you miss a day, you don't quit; you just start again the next day."

BLOCK 4: PRACTICE (One Habit This Week)

Habit: The "Trigger" Habit.

When we'll do it: Pick something you already do every day (like brushing teeth or putting on shoes). We will attach a tiny prayer to it. (Example: "When I put on my shoes, I pray, 'God, walk with me today.'")

What to watch for: Seeing how easy it is to add God into our day when we attach it to something we already do.

Prayer: Lord, help us to build a life that honors You, not just in big moments but in our small, daily choices. Give us the self-control to train our hearts to love You. Amen.

BLOCK 5: PARENT NOTES (The Secret Weapon)

The Doctrine, Precisely This week focuses on the *spiritual disciplines* (or means of grace). We are moving from "trying" to "training." We cannot expect to act like Jesus in a crisis if we do not practice the lifestyle of Jesus in our everyday moments.

A habit is simply a rhythm of grace. We don't do these things to *earn* God's love (that is legalism); we do them to *place ourselves in the way* of God's love (that is discipline). Just as a sail doesn't create the wind but catches it, spiritual habits position our hearts to catch the wind of the Spirit.

Why It Matters

- **It bypasses willpower:** Willpower is a limited resource (like a battery). Habits are automatic. If we have to decide every single morning *if* we will read the Bible, we will often fail. If it is a habit, we just do it.

- **It shapes identity:** Every small action is like a vote for the type of person you are becoming.

- **It creates safety:** Family habits (like dinner together or night prayer) create a sense of stability and belonging for children.

Common Misunderstandings to Avoid

- **Misunderstanding:** Spiritual disciplines make me a "super Christian."

  ○ **Correction:** They are basic maintenance, like eating and sleeping. They are for every believer, not just the elite.

- **Misunderstanding:** If I miss a day, I've failed.

  ○ **Correction:** The goal is trajectory, not perfection. This is a "grace-based" approach to habits.

How to Answer Follow-Up Questions If they ask: "Why can't I just pray when I feel like it?" **Say:** "Because our feelings change like the weather. If you only ate when you felt like it, you might get sick. We pray to keep our relationship strong even when we don't feel 'spiritual.'"

If they ask: "Is God mad if I forget to read my Bible?" **Say:** "No. God loves you because of Jesus, not because of your reading streak. But He misses talking with you, and you miss out on His wisdom when you skip it."

Extra Bible Anchors for Parents 1 Corinthians 9:24–27; Galatians 6:9; Hebrews 12:1–2 1 Timothy 4:7 , "But have nothing to do with pointless and silly myths. Rather, train yourself in godliness." (CSB)

Teach-It-Back Prompt The "Toothbrush Challenge." Tonight while brushing teeth, ask: "Why do we do this every single night?" (To stop cavities/decay). Say: "Just like brushing stops cavities, reading the Bible stops lies from sticking to our hearts."

<u>MEMORY (One-Liner + Catechism Q/A)</u>

One-Liner: Spiritual habits train our hearts to love God.

Optional Q&A: Q: Why do we have spiritual habits? A: To help us grow in godliness and stay close to Jesus.

<u>Notes:</u>

PART 2: God the Father

N ow that we've got our footing, we lift our eyes to **Who God is**. In this section we'll explore the **Trinity**, God's **attributes** (like holiness and love), and **creation.**

Not as abstract ideas, but as truths your kids can actually lean on. Small views of God create big fears.

A big, sturdy view of God becomes a **safe harbor** for a child's heart.

Week by week, we're going to replace fuzzy "God is kind of like…" thoughts with clear, beautiful, biblical clarity.

As you move through the pages, watch for a quiet shift: your kids start to feel safer… not because life gets easier, but because they're learning exactly **Who is in charge of the universe** (and that He is good).

WEEK 10: GOD'S CHARACTER

BLOCK 1: KID PAGE (Big Idea + Anchor Verse)

Big Idea God is not just big and powerful; He is perfectly good, holy, and loving in everything He does. We never have to guess what God is like because He has shown us His character clearly in the Bible and in Jesus. Because God is good all the time, we can trust Him even when life feels confusing.

Anchor Verse Exodus 34:6

In Kid Words "The Lord passed in front of Moses and said: I am the Lord! I am a God who is kind and tender. I don't get angry quickly. I am overflowing with faithful love and truth."

Key Words

- **Character:** The set of qualities that makes someone who they are (like being honest, kind, or brave).

- **Holy:** Totally perfect, set apart, and without any sin or darkness.

- **Faithful:** Someone who keeps their promises and never gives up on you.

More Bible places to look: Psalm 100:5; Psalm 145:17; 1 John 1:5; Isaiah 6:3; Nahum 1:7

BLOCK 2: STORY PAGE (Real Life Scenario)

Story Title: The Whisper in the Hallway

Setting: The crowded hallway outside the cafeteria right before lunch. It was loud, chaotic, and smelled like floor wax.

Problem: Maya was walking with her friend, Chloe, when Chloe leaned in close, covering her mouth with her hand. "Did you hear about Sarah?" Chloe whispered, her eyes wide with excitement. "I heard she failed the math test because she tried to cheat. Everyone is talking about it." Maya knew Sarah. Sarah was quiet and nice. Maya also knew that Sarah had been out sick for three days, which was probably why she struggled with the test.

Choice Moment: Maya felt a little thrill, it felt good to know a secret. She wanted Chloe to keep liking her. She could nod and say, "No way, really?" and pass it on. Or, she could stop the rumor right there.

Small Resolution: Maya took a breath. "I don't think she cheated, Chloe. She was sick all week. That doesn't sound like her." Chloe shrugged, looking a little disappointed. "Whatever." The conversation died out, but Maya felt a heavy weight lift off her chest.

Quick Takeaway: God is Truth and Love, so when we stop a lie or refuse to gossip, we are acting like Him.

BLOCK 3: TALK-IT-OUT (Discussion + Coaching)

1. **Understanding:** In the story, why was it hard for Maya to tell the truth instead of just listening to the rumor?

2. **Connection:** How is gossip (saying mean or untrue things behind someone's back) the opposite of God's character?

3. **Application:** Is there anyone at school or on your team who people are mean to? How can you show them God's kindness this week?

If your kid says: "But what if the rumor is true?" **Try:** "Even if it is true, does sharing it help that person or hurt them? God is full of truth, but He is also full of love. He doesn't use truth to embarrass people."

If your kid says: "God doesn't feel good to me right now because something bad happened." **Try:** "I hear you. That is really hard. But God's character doesn't change just because our situation hurts. He is good, even when life is bad. We can tell Him we are hurt, and He will listen."

BLOCK 4: PRACTICE (One Habit This Week)

The Habit: The "Is It True?" Filter

When We'll Do It: Whenever we are about to talk about someone who isn't in the room (at dinner, in the car, or texting).

What to Watch For: Notice how often we want to say something negative about someone else just to be funny or interesting. Catch yourself and stop.

Short Prayer: "God, You are perfect and good. Please guard my mouth today. Help me to speak words that are true and kind, just like You."

BLOCK 5: PARENT NOTES (The Secret Weapon)

The Doctrine: God's Communicable Attributes We often focus on God's power (He is all-knowing, all-powerful). Those are attributes we *don't* share with Him. But this week is about His moral character, attributes we *can* share (imperfectly). God is Holy, Just, Good, True, and Loving. He isn't just "loving" sometimes; He *is* Love. He isn't just "truthful" when it's convenient; He *is* Truth.

Because God is personal, we don't worship a generic "force." We worship a Person with a specific personality. The beauty of the Gospel is that while we fail at being good, God never does. And through Jesus, He is slowly shaping us to look like the family portrait again.

Why It Matters

- **It builds trust.** If God were all-powerful but not good, He would be a terrifying tyrant. Because He is good, we can trust His power.

- **It sets the standard.** We don't define "good" based on our feelings or culture. We define "good" by looking at God.

- **It gives us a goal.** We are created in His image, which means we are designed to reflect His kindness, truth, and faithfulness to the world.

Common Misunderstandings to Avoid

- **Misunderstanding**: God is happy when I'm good and angry when I'm bad.

    - **Correction**: God's character is unchangeable. He doesn't wake up grumpy. His love for His children is steady, settled, and constant.

- **Misunderstanding**: God is nice and never judges sin.

    - **Correction**: God is simple, meaning all His attributes work together. He is Loving, but He is also Holy and Just. He cannot love sin because sin hurts the people He loves.

- **Misunderstanding:** We can be exactly like God.

    - **Correction**: We reflect Him, like a mirror reflects the sun. The mirror isn't the sun, but it shines with the same light. We are imperfect; He is the source.

Scripts for Hard Questions

- **Q: "If God is good, why do bad things happen?"**

    - A: "That is the biggest question in the world. We know the world is broken because of sin, and God hates that brokenness too. But we know He is good because He didn't leave us alone in it, He sent Jesus to fix it. We trust His heart even when we can't see His hand."

- **Q: "Does God have a personality?"**

    - A: "Yes! He isn't a robot or a cloud. He thinks, feels, loves, and decides. The best way to see God's personality is to look at Jesus."

- **Q: "Is God strictly serious all the time?"**

    - A: "Well, He invented platypuses, laughter, and taste buds. I think God is full of joy."

Extra Bible Anchors: Psalm 34:8; 1 Peter 1:15–16; James 1:17

Teach-It-Back (30 Seconds) "Imagine you have a friend who thinks God is mean and scary, like a bully in the sky. Based on what we learned, what is one thing you could tell them about what God is really like?"

MEMORY (One-Liner + Catechism Q/A)

One-Liner God is perfectly good, holy, and loving, and He never changes.

Catechism Q: What is God? **A:** God is a Spirit, infinite, eternal, and unchangeable in his being, wisdom, power, holiness, justice, goodness, and truth. (Westminster Shorter Catechism Q.4)

Notes:

WEEK 11: THE TRINITY

BLOCK 1: KID PAGE (Big Idea + Anchor Verse)

Big Idea There is only one God, but He exists in three Persons: God the Father, God the Son (Jesus), and God the Holy Spirit. This is a mystery that is hard for our brains to understand, but it is true. Because God has always been Father, Son, and Spirit, He has never been lonely, He is love in His very nature.

Anchor Verse Matthew 28:19

In Kid Words "Jesus told us to go tell everyone about Him, welcoming them into the family of the Father, the Son, and the Holy Spirit."

Key Words

- **Trinity:** The word we use to say God is "Three in One."

- **Person:** Not a human person, but a distinct center of thinking, willing, and loving within the one true God.

- **Unity:** Being one or joined together perfectly.

More Bible places to look: Deuteronomy 6:4; Matthew 3:16–17; 2 Corinthians 13:13; John 1:1–2; Genesis 1:26

BLOCK 2: STORY PAGE (Real Life Scenario)

Story Title: The Loud Question in the Quiet Church

Setting: Sitting in the middle pew at church on Sunday morning. The pastor was talking, and it was very quiet.

Problem: The pastor said, "God sent His Son..." and 8-year-old Liam's brow furrowed. He leaned over to his dad and whispered, way too loudly, "Wait, if God is Jesus's dad, are there two Gods? Or three with the Spirit guy? How does that work?" A lady in the row in front of them turned around and smiled (mostly nicely). Liam slumped in his seat, feeling like he asked a dumb question.

Choice Moment: Liam felt embarrassed. He could decide church was too confusing and just draw on the bulletin. Or, he could ask his dad about it later, even if it seemed complicated.

Small Resolution: In the car ride home, Dad didn't laugh. "That was a great question, Liam," he said. "It's actually the biggest mystery in the universe. We believe in one God, but three Persons. It's like God is a perfect family of love all by Himself." Liam nodded. He didn't totally get it, but he was glad he wasn't "wrong."

Quick Takeaway: The Trinity is a big mystery, but it reminds us that God is Love.

BLOCK 3: TALK-IT-OUT (Discussion + Coaching)

1. **Understanding:** Why was Liam confused in the story? Have you ever wondered how God can be three and one at the same time?

2. **Connection:** If God were just one person all alone before He made the world, who would He have loved? (The Trinity means God has always loved the Father, Son, and Spirit).

3. **Application:** The Trinity works together perfectly. How can our family work together like a team this week?

If your kid says: "Is God like an egg? Or water?" (Common analogies). **Try:** "Those are clever ideas, but they actually don't quite work. An egg shell isn't the yolk, but the Father *is* God and the Son *is* God. It's better to say: There is nothing else like God. He is unique."

If your kid says: "It makes my brain hurt." **Try:** "Me too! If we could totally understand God, He would be small enough to fit in our pockets. The fact that He is bigger than our brains is a good thing, it means He is big enough to save us."

BLOCK 4: PRACTICE (One Habit This Week)

The Habit: The Doxology (A Song of Praise)

When We'll Do It: Before bed one night this week, or in the car.

What to Watch For: Listen for the three names of God.

Short Prayer: "Glory be to the Father, and to the Son, and to the Holy Spirit. As it was in the beginning, is now, and ever shall be, world without end. Amen."

BLOCK 5: PARENT NOTES (The Secret Weapon)

The Doctrine: The Trinity This is the distinctively Christian view of God. We are monotheists (one God), not polytheists (many gods). Yet, Scripture clearly shows the Father is God, Jesus is God, and the Spirit is God.

- **The Father** plans and sends.

- **The Son** accomplishes redemption.

- **The Spirit** applies it to our hearts. They are co-equal and co-eternal.

Why It Matters

- **God is Love:** If God were a single person (unitarian), He would have needed to create the world to have someone to love. Because God is Triune, He has *always* been loving within Himself. He didn't create us because He was lonely; He created us to share His overflowing joy.

- **Salvation:** If Jesus isn't fully God, He can't save us. If the Spirit isn't fully God, He can't give us new life.

Common Misunderstandings to Avoid

- **Misunderstanding:** "Three Gods working together." (Tritheism)

  - **Correction:** There is only ONE divine being. They share one will and essence.

- **Misunderstanding:** "God wears three masks." (Modalism)

  - **Correction:** This is the idea that God is sometimes the Father, then switches to being the Son. But at Jesus's baptism, all three are there at once (Voice, Son, Dove). They are distinct persons, not just "modes."

Scripts for Hard Questions

- **Q: "Who is the boss in the Trinity?"**

  - A: "They are all equal in glory and power. But they have different roles. The Son loves to do the Father's will, and the Spirit loves to shine the spotlight on the Son. They serve one another perfectly."

- **Q: "Can I pray to the Holy Spirit?"**

  - A: "Yes! You can pray to any Person of the Trinity. Usually, the Bible shows us praying to the Father, in the name of Jesus, by the power of the Spirit. But talking to any of them is talking to God."

Extra Bible Anchors: John 14:16–17; Ephesians 1:3–14 (Note the roles of Father, Son, Spirit)

Teach-It-Back (30 Seconds) "If someone asked you, 'Do Christians believe in three gods?', what would you say?" (Answer: No, one God in three Persons.)

MEMORY (One-Liner + Catechism Q/A)

One-Line Definition There is one God in three Persons: Father, Son, and Holy Spirit.

Q/A Q: How many persons are there in God? **A:** There are three persons in the one true God: the Father, the Son, and the Holy Spirit.

Notes:

WEEK 12: CREATION

BLOCK 1: KID PAGE (Big Idea + Anchor Verse)

Big Idea God created everything that exists out of nothing, simply by speaking His word. Because God made the world, it belongs to Him. And because He made you on purpose, your value comes from Him, not from what you own or how you look.

Anchor Verse Genesis 1:1

In Kid Words "In the beginning, God created the heavens and the earth."

Key Words

- **Creator:** The one who makes something. (God is the Creator; we are creatures).

- **Ex Nihilo:** A fancy Latin phrase meaning "out of nothing." God didn't use Legos or clay; He made the materials too.

More Bible places to look: Psalm 19:1; John 1:3; Hebrews 11:3; Psalm 139:13–14; Colossians 1:16

BLOCK 2: STORY PAGE (Real Life Scenario)

Story Title: The "Cool" Outfit

Setting: The mall with Mom, looking for back-to-school clothes.

Problem: Jackson saw the hoodie in the window. It was the exact one all the popular kids at the skate park were wearing. It had the "bolt" logo on the sleeve. But when he looked at the price tag, his stomach dropped. It was way too expensive. "Mom, I *need* this," Jackson pleaded. "If I wear my old stuff, I'm going to look like a nobody."

Choice Moment: Jackson felt like his whole reputation depended on that hoodie. He could get angry and beg, believing the lie that his value was in the logo. Or, he could remember who made him.

Small Resolution: Mom put a hand on his shoulder. "We can't get that one, bud. But remember, the logo doesn't make you cool. You're cool because God made you." Jackson sighed. He was still bummed, but he put the hoodie back. He realized the kid inside the hoodie mattered more than the fabric on the outside.

Quick Takeaway: What we wear doesn't give us value; being made by God does.

BLOCK 3: TALK-IT-OUT (Discussion + Coaching)

1. **Understanding:** Why did Jackson feel like he "needed" that specific hoodie?

2. **Connection:** How does knowing God made you change how you feel when you don't have the "coolest" stuff?

3. **Application:** What is one thing you like about how God made you? (It could be your laugh, your ability to run fast, or your kindness).

If your kid says: "But I really DO look weird compared to everyone else." **Try:** "It's hard when we feel different. But God doesn't make mistakes. He designed you on purpose. The things that make you different are often the things He uses to do special work."

If your kid says: "Did God make mosquitoes? Why?" **Try:** "Yes, He made everything! Originally, everything was good. Some things became pesty or scary after the world broke (sin), but every creature still shows how creative God is."

BLOCK 4: PRACTICE (One Habit This Week)

The Habit: The "Wow" Walk

When We'll Do It: Take a 5-minute walk outside or look out the window.

What to Watch For: Find one thing God made that is tiny (an ant, a leaf) and one thing that is huge (the sky, a tree).

Short Prayer: "God, You are the great Creator. Thank You for making this world and for making me. Help me to take care of Your creation."

BLOCK 5: PARENT NOTES (The Secret Weapon)

The Doctrine: Creation God is distinct from His creation. He isn't the trees or the wind (that's pantheism); He *made* the trees and the wind. This means the universe has a Owner. We are stewards, not owners.

Why It Matters

- **Identity:** If we are accidents of biology, our value is based on our performance or popularity. If we are created by God, our value is built-in and unchangeable.

- **Purpose:** You don't buy a toaster to use it as a hammer. You use it for what the designer intended. To find our purpose, we must look to our Designer.

Common Misunderstandings to Avoid

- **Misunderstanding:** "Science and faith are enemies."

  - **Correction:** Science studies *how* the world works; theology studies *Who* made it and *why*. They are friends. God gave us brains to explore His world.

- **Misunderstanding:** "God needed us."

  - **Correction:** God didn't create because He was bored or needy. He created out of freedom and generosity.

Scripts for Hard Questions

- **Q: "How did God make the world in six days?"**

  - A: "The Bible says 'six days,' and Christians have different ideas about what that looked like. Some think they were 24-hour days like ours; others think they were long periods of time. The most important part isn't *how long* it took, but *Who* did it."

- **Q: "Who made God?"**

  - A: "Nobody! That's what makes Him God. Everything else had a beginning, but God has always been there. He is the Uncreated One."

Extra Bible Anchors: Acts 17:24–25; Revelation 4:11

Teach-It-Back (30 Seconds) "Look at your hand. Wiggle your fingers. Who designed that? (God). Does that mean you are valuable even if you have a bad day? (Yes)."

<u>MEMORY (One-Liner + Catechism Q/A)</u>

One-Line Definition God created everything from nothing simply by speaking.

Q/A Q: Who made you and all things? **A:** God made me and all things for His own glory.

<u>Notes:</u>

WEEK 13: PROVIDENCE

BLOCK 1: KID PAGE (Big Idea + Anchor Verse)

Big Idea God didn't just create the world and then walk away. He holds everything together and takes care of His creation every single second. This is called "Providence." It means God is involved in the big things (like planets spinning) and the small things (like you losing a tooth).

Anchor Verse Romans 8:28

In Kid Words "We know that all things work together for the good of those who love God, who are called according to His purpose."

Key Words

- **Providence:** God's "pro-vision" (seeing beforehand) and care for the world.

- **Sustain:** To keep something going. (Like a battery sustains a flashlight).

- **Sovereign:** God is the King and has the right to rule over everything.

More Bible places to look: Matthew 6:26; Matthew 10:29–31; Colossians 1:17; Psalm 104:14; Proverbs 16:9

BLOCK 2: STORY PAGE (Real Life Scenario)

Story Title: The Lost Allowance Money

Setting: The messy bedroom floor, surrounded by piles of laundry and toys.

Problem: Lucas had saved his allowance for three weeks to buy a new graphic novel. He kept the $15 in an envelope on his desk. But today, the envelope was gone. He checked his drawers. He checked under the bed. Nothing. His chest started to feel tight. "It's gone!" he yelled. "I lost it forever!"

Choice Moment: Lucas felt total panic. He could scream and blame his little sister (even though she wasn't in his room). Or, he could stop, take a breath, and ask God for help, trusting that God cares about his $15.

Small Resolution: Lucas sat down. "God, I'm really upset. Please help me find it. And if I can't, help me be okay." He didn't find it right away. But later that afternoon, his dad found the envelope tucked inside a library book Lucas had returned. Even before he got the money back, Lucas felt calmer because he knew he wasn't alone.

Quick Takeaway: We can talk to God about everything because He cares about the details of our lives.

<u>BLOCK 3: TALK-IT-OUT (Discussion + Coaching)</u>

1. **Understanding:** Why did Lucas panic? Do you ever feel like God doesn't care about your small problems?

2. **Connection:** How is God "sustaining" (holding up) the world right now? (Sun rising, gravity working, your heart beating).

3. **Application:** Is there something you are worried about today? Let's practice giving it to God.

If your kid says: "But I prayed for my lost toy and never found it." **Try:** "That is really disappointing. God isn't a genie who grants every wish. But Providence means He gives us what we *need*, even if it's not always what we *want*. He is teaching us to trust Him more than our stuff."

If your kid says: "Does God control robots?" **Try:** "He is in charge of everything! But He usually lets things work according to how He made them. He lets gravity work, and He lets computers work. But He can intervene anytime He wants."

<u>BLOCK 4: PRACTICE (One Habit This Week)</u>

The Habit: The "Bird Check"

When We'll Do It: Whenever you see a bird outside this week.

What to Watch For: Remember Jesus said God feeds the birds. If He cares for them, He cares for you.

Short Prayer: "God, You hold the whole world in Your hands. Thank You for taking care of me today."

<u>BLOCK 5: PARENT NOTES (The Secret Weapon)</u>

The Doctrine: Providence This doctrine answers the question: "Is God involved?" Deism says God made the world like a watch, wound it up, and left it on a shelf. The Bible says God is actively involved in sustaining and governing all things.

Why It Matters

- **Antidote to Anxiety:** If the universe is random, we should be terrified. If a good Father is in control, we can sleep at night.

- **Meaning in Pain:** Romans 8:28 doesn't say "everything is good." It says God works *in* all things (even bad ones) *for* good. He wastes nothing.

Common Misunderstandings to Avoid

- **Misunderstanding:** "Everything that happens is God's 'will' in the same way."

  - **Correction:** God allows sin, but He doesn't cause it or love it. We say God "permits" bad choices but "ordains" the final outcome for His glory.

- **Misunderstanding:** "I don't need to look both ways before crossing the street because God protects me."

  - **Correction:** God usually works *through* means (like wisdom, seatbelts, and doctors). Acting foolishly is not trusting God; it's testing Him.

Scripts for Hard Questions

- **Q: "Does God decide who wins the Super Bowl?"**

  - A: "God is in charge of everything, so nothing happens without His permission. But usually, He lets the team that plays better win. He cares more about the players' hearts than the score."

- **Q: "Why didn't God stop me from scraping my knee?"**

  - A: "God doesn't put us in a bubble wrap suit. He lets us learn from the world, and sometimes that means we fall. But He is always there to comfort us and heal us."

Extra Bible Anchors: Genesis 50:20 (Joseph's story); Acts 17:28

Teach-It-Back (30 Seconds) "Hold up a pencil and let it drop. Why did it fall? (Gravity). Who keeps gravity working every second? (God). That's Providence!"

MEMORY (One-Liner + Catechism Q/A)

One-Line Definition God upholds the world and guides all things for His purpose.

Q/A Q: What is God's providence? **A:** It is God's holy, wise, and powerful care for everything He has made.

Notes:

WEEK 14: GOD'S PRESENCE

BLOCK 1: KID PAGE (Big Idea + Anchor Verse)

Big Idea God is "omnipresent," which means He is everywhere all the time. You cannot go anywhere where God is not. But for His children, He is present in a special way, He is *with* us as a Friend, Helper, and Father. You are never, ever truly alone.

Anchor Verse Psalm 139:7–10

In Kid Words "There is nowhere I can run where God isn't already there. Even if I go up to the sky or hide in the dark, God is right beside me."

Key Words

- **Omnipresent:** Present everywhere at the same time.

- **Comfort:** Feeling safe and peaceful because someone is with you.

More Bible places to look: Matthew 28:20; Joshua 1:9; Jeremiah 23:23–24; Hebrews 13:5

BLOCK 2: STORY PAGE (Real Life Scenario)

Story Title: Lonely Recess

Setting: The edge of the playground, near the chain-link fence.

Problem: Mia's best friend was sick, and her other friends were playing a game of tag that they said was "full." Mia stood by herself, kicking at the woodchips. She watched everyone else laughing and running. She felt invisible. A lump formed in her throat. *No one sees me,* she thought. *I'm all by myself.*

Choice Moment: The sadness felt like a heavy blanket. Mia could go hide in the bathroom until recess was over. Or, she could remember what they talked about at dinner, that God is always right there.

Small Resolution: Mia whispered, "God, I feel lonely. Please be with me." Nothing magical happened, the sky didn't open up. But she remembered the truth deep inside: *God sees me.* * She took a deep breath, walked over to the swings, and started swinging. A few minutes later, a girl from another class came over. "Want a push?" she asked.

Quick Takeaway: Even when we feel invisible to people, we are never invisible to God.

BLOCK 3: TALK-IT-OUT (Discussion + Coaching)

1. **Understanding:** How did talking to God help Mia even before the other girl came over?

2. **Connection:** Have you ever felt lonely at school or at home? Does it help to know God is sitting right there with you?

3. **Application:** Since God is everywhere, that means He is with us when we are scared in the dark, and when we are taking a hard test. Let's list places where God is.

If your kid says: "Is God in the bathroom?" **Try:** (Don't laugh!) "Yes, God is everywhere! That means He isn't grossed out by being human. He made our bodies. There is no place where we have to hide from Him."

If your kid says: "I talked to God but I didn't feel Him." **Try:** "That is normal. Feelings come and go, like clouds. The truth is like the sun, it's there even behind the clouds. We believe God is there because He promised, not just because we get goosebumps."

BLOCK 4: PRACTICE (One Habit This Week)

The Habit: The Empty Chair

When We'll Do It: At dinner or while watching a movie.

What to Watch For: Imagine Jesus is sitting in the empty chair in the room. He is listening to our conversation. How does that change what we say?

Short Prayer: "God, thank You for being here right now. Thank You that I never have to be alone."

BLOCK 5: PARENT NOTES (The Secret Weapon)

The Doctrine: Omnipresence God is infinite spirit; He is not limited by space. He is fully present in every point of space with His whole being.

Why It Matters

- **Restraint for Sin:** Knowing God sees everything stops us from doing things in secret.

- **Comfort for Suffering:** Knowing God is *with* us changes how we endure pain. We can handle almost anything if we know we aren't alone.

Common Misunderstandings to Avoid

- **Misunderstanding:** "God is 'in' the trees like a force." (Pantheism)

    - **Correction**: God is *present* with the tree, sustaining it, but He is not *the* tree. He is distinct from creation.

- **Misunderstanding:** "God is only at church."

    - **Correction**: God is specially present among His people gathered for worship, but He doesn't stay in the building when we leave. He goes with us.

Scripts for Hard Questions

- **Q: "If God is everywhere, is He in hell?"**

    - A: "That's a heavy question. The Bible suggests God is present in hell as a Judge, but His *relational presence*, His kindness, comfort, and friendship, is absent. Hell is a place without God's goodness."

- **Q: "Can I hide from God?"**

    - A: "Jonah tried! But he found out you can't. And that is actually good news. It means God can find you no matter how lost you get."

Extra Bible Anchors: Psalm 23:4 ("You are with me"); Acts 17:27

Teach-It-Back (30 Seconds) "If you were an astronaut on Mars, would God be there? (Yes). If you were in a submarine at the bottom of the ocean? (Yes). Is He here right now? (Yes!)."

MEMORY (One-Liner + Catechism Q/A)

One-Line Definition God is fully present everywhere, so I am never alone.

Q/A Q: Where is God? **A:** God is everywhere.

Notes:

WEEK 15: REVIEW: THE GOD MAP

BLOCK 1: KID PAGE (Big Idea + Anchor Verse)

Big Idea We have learned so much about God! He is Good, Holy, Three-in-One, the Creator, and the Provider. When we forget who God is, we get scared, angry, or confused. But when we use our "God Map" (the truths we've learned), we can find our way back to peace and joy.

Anchor Verse Psalm 86:11

In Kid Words "Teach me your way, Lord, and I will live by your truth. Give me an undivided mind to fear your name."

Key Words

- **Review:** Looking back at what we learned so we don't forget.

- **Trust:** Relying on God because we know His character.

More Bible places to look: Psalm 9:10; Proverbs 18:10

BLOCK 2: STORY PAGE (Real Life Scenario)

Story Title: The Dinner Table Outburst

Setting: The dinner table. Mom made meatloaf (again).

Problem: Everything had gone wrong for Eli today. He forgot his homework, he tripped at recess, and now there were peas touching his meatloaf. "I hate this!" Eli shouted, slamming his fork down. "Everything is stupid!" The whole table went silent.

Choice Moment: Eli knew he was out of control. He felt angry and embarrassed. His dad looked at him calmly. "Eli, let's take a breath," Dad said. "It sounds like you're having a hard day. Let's look at our God Map. Is God still good today?"

Small Resolution: Eli crossed his arms. "Doesn't feel like it." Dad nodded. "I know. But is He?" Eli sighed. "Yes. He's still good. And He's still in charge." Just saying it out loud made the anger bubble shrink a little. "Sorry I yelled," Eli mumbled. "Can I have some ketchup?"

Quick Takeaway: When we are angry or upset, remembering who God is helps us hit "reset."

BLOCK 3: TALK-IT-OUT (Discussion + Coaching)

1. **Understanding:** How did remembering God help Eli calm down?

2. **Connection:** Which attribute of God (Good, Holy, Creator, Provider, Present) means the most to you right now?

3. **Application:** Let's practice. If you are scared of the dark tonight, which truth about God helps? (He is Present).

If your kid says: "I forgot everything we learned." **Try:** "That's okay! That's why we review. Let's just remember one thing: God is Good. Can you say that?"

- **If your kid says:** "Does God get mad when I have an outburst?" **Try:** "God loves honesty. He wants you to tell Him when you're mad. But He also wants to help you act like Jesus, who had self-control."

BLOCK 4: PRACTICE (One Habit This Week)

The Habit: The Attribute Match Game

When We'll Do It: During a car ride or breakfast.

What to Watch For: Match a problem to a truth.

- Scared -> God is Present.

- Need something -> God is Provider.

- Confused -> God is Truth.

- **Short Prayer:** "God, thank You for being exactly who You are. Keep these truths deep in my heart."

BLOCK 5: PARENT NOTES (The Secret Weapon)

The Doctrine: Review & Integration This week is a "catch-up" week. We aren't adding new info; we are cementing the foundation. Repetition is the mother of learning.

Why It Matters

- **Theology is for Life:** If theology stays in our heads, it makes us proud. If it moves to our hearts, it makes us humble and peaceful. We want kids to use these truths as tools.

Common Misunderstandings to Avoid

- **Misunderstanding:** "We learned it once, so we know it."

  - **Correction:** We leak. We need to hear the Gospel and the truths of God over and over again.

Scripts for Hard Questions

- **Q: "Why do we have to talk about God so much?"**

  - A: "Because everything else in the world is talking to us too, TV, friends, school. They tell us what matters. We talk about God to remember what is *really* true."

Extra Bible Anchors: Deuteronomy 6:6–9 (Talk about them when you sit, walk, lie down, rise).

Teach-It-Back (30 Seconds) "High five! Tell me one thing about God you learned in the last few weeks."

MEMORY (One-Liner + Catechism Q/A)

One-Line Definition We remember God's truth so we can trust Him in real life.

Q/A Q: What is the first and greatest commandment? **A:** To love the Lord your God with all your heart, soul, mind, and strength.

Notes:

WEEK 16: LIFE SKILL: WORSHIP

BLOCK 1: KID PAGE (Big Idea + Anchor Verse)

Big Idea Worship isn't just singing songs at church. Worship is giving God the honor and love He deserves with your whole life. We worship God when we thank Him, when we obey Him, and when we enjoy the good things He has given us.

Anchor Verse Romans 12:1

In Kid Words "Brothers and sisters... present your bodies as a living sacrifice, holy and pleasing to God; this is your true worship."

Key Words

- **Worship:** Showing God how much He is worth to us.

- **Gratitude:** Being thankful for what we have instead of complaining about what we don't have.

More Bible places to look: Psalm 100:1–2; Psalm 95:6; John 4:23–24; Colossians 3:16

BLOCK 2: STORY PAGE (Real Life Scenario)

Story Title: The Thankfulness Challenge

Setting: Saturday morning chores. The house was messy.

Problem: "Ugh, why do I always have to unload the dishwasher?" Sophie groaned. "It's so unfair. Ben never does anything!" She slammed a plate onto the counter. She was in a grumbling mood. The cereal was soggy, the TV remote was lost, and everything was annoying.

Choice Moment: Dad walked in. "Sounds like a Grumble Storm is hitting," he smiled. "Sophie, you can keep complaining, which makes the work feel harder. Or, we can try a Worship Challenge. For every dish you put away, say one thing you're thankful for."

Small Resolution: Sophie rolled her eyes at first. "I'm thankful for... plates?" she mumbled. Dad chuckled. "Counts." "I'm thankful for... pizza." "I'm thankful for... my soccer team." By the time the dishwasher was empty, Sophie wasn't grumbling anymore. She was actually smiling.

Quick Takeaway: When we switch from complaining to thanking, we turn our work into worship.

BLOCK 3: TALK-IT-OUT (Discussion + Coaching)

1. **Understanding:** How did being thankful change Sophie's mood?

2. **Connection:** Why does God like it when we say "thank you"? (It shows we know He is the Giver of good gifts).

3. **Application:** What is one thing you usually complain about? (Homework, chores, bedtime). How can you worship God in that thing?

If your kid says: "Do I have to sing to worship?" **Try:** "Nope! Singing is a great way to worship, but you can also worship by sharing your toys, telling the truth, or doing your best in school."

If your kid says: "I don't feel thankful today." **Try:** "That's honest. Sometimes worship is a choice, not a feeling. We say 'Thank You God' even when we are sad, because He is still good."

BLOCK 4: PRACTICE (One Habit This Week)

The Habit: The "Thank You" Loop

When We'll Do It: At the end of the day.

What to Watch For: Name 3 things that happened today that were good. Say "Thank You God for [Item 1]" for each one.

Short Prayer: "God, You are worthy of all my praise. Help me to worship You with my lips and my life today."

BLOCK 5: PARENT NOTES (The Secret Weapon)

The Doctrine: Worship as Life We often compartmentalize "worship" to Sunday morning music. But biblically, worship is a "posture of the heart" directed toward God. Romans 12:1 calls it a "living sacrifice."

Why It Matters

- **Combats Entitlement:** Our culture teaches kids they deserve everything. Worship teaches them that everything is a gift of grace.

- **Joy:** A worshipping heart is a joyful heart. A complaining heart is miserable.

Common Misunderstandings to Avoid

- **Misunderstanding:** "Worship is for the adults."

    ○ **Correction:** Jesus quoted Psalm 8:2, saying that praise comes from the lips of children and infants. Kids are natural worshippers.

- **Misunderstanding:** "I only worship when I'm at church."

    ○ **Correction:** You are always worshipping something (comfort, approval, fun). The goal is to direct that worship to God.

Scripts for Hard Questions

- **Q: "Why does God want us to praise Him? Does He have a big ego?"**

    ○ A: "Great question. God doesn't *need* our praise to feel good about Himself. He wants us to praise Him because *it is good for us.* Just like you naturally cheer when your team scores, we are built to cheer for what is greatest. Praising God completes our joy."

Extra Bible Anchors: 1 Chronicles 16:29; Psalm 150:6

Teach-It-Back (30 Seconds) "If you share your snack with a friend because you love Jesus, is that worship? (Yes!)"

<u>MEMORY (One-Liner + Catechism Q/A)</u>

One-Line Definition Worship is honoring God with our words, our work, and our hearts.

Q/A Q: Why did God make you? **A:** God made me to glorify Him and enjoy Him forever.

<u>Notes:</u>

WEEK 17: LIFE SKILL: TRUST WHEN YOU CAN'T SEE

BLOCK 1: KID PAGE (Big Idea + Anchor Verse)

Big Idea Sometimes the world looks scary. We see bad news or feel afraid of what might happen. Trusting God doesn't mean we pretend everything is fine. It means we believe God is bigger than the scary things, and He has a plan even when we can't see it yet.

Anchor Verse Proverbs 3:5–6

In Kid Words "Trust God with your whole heart instead of thinking you know everything. Invite Him into every part of your day, and He will show you where to go."

Key Words

- **Trust:** Believing someone is telling the truth and will take care of you.

- **Understanding:** What our brains can figure out on their own (which is limited!).

More Bible places to look: Psalm 56:3; Isaiah 26:3; Mark 4:39–40; Psalm 46:1

BLOCK 2: STORY PAGE (Real Life Scenario)

Story Title: The News Fear Spiral

Setting: The living room. The TV news was on in the background.

Problem: Caleb was playing with Legos, but he heard the reporter talking about a "crisis" and "danger." He looked up and saw pictures of people running. His stomach did a flip-flop. Later, in bed, he couldn't sleep. His mind started racing: *What if that happens here? What if something happens to Mom?*

Choice Moment: The fear felt like a dark cloud. Caleb could lie there and let the "What If" monster grow bigger. Or, he could turn on the "Trust Light."

Small Resolution: He called out, "Mom?" When she came in, he told her about the scary news. She sat on his bed. "That is scary stuff, Caleb. It's okay to feel sad about it. But remember who is the King of the world?" "God is," Caleb said. "Right. Even when things are shaking, God is solid like a rock. We can pray for those people, and then trust God to keep us."

Quick Takeaway: When we are afraid, we can trade our "What Ifs" for "God Is."

BLOCK 3: TALK-IT-OUT (Discussion + Coaching)

1. **Understanding:** What made Caleb scared? Have you ever heard something on the news or at school that scared you?

2. **Connection:** How is God like a "rock" when things are scary? (He doesn't move; He is strong).

3. **Application:** Let's memorize a short sentence for when we feel afraid: "When I am afraid, I will trust in You."

If your kid says: "But bad things DO happen to Christians." **Try:** "That is true. Trusting God doesn't mean nothing bad will ever happen. It means that *if* something bad happens, God will be right there with us to help us through it. We are never alone."

If your kid says: "I can't stop worrying." **Try:** "Worry is like a sticky trap. Let's try to 'change the channel' in your brain. Let's list three things we know are true about God."

BLOCK 4: PRACTICE (One Habit This Week)

The Habit: The "Cast Your Cares" Throw

When We'll Do It: If you feel worried.

What to Watch For: Pretend you are holding a heavy rock (your worry). Imagine throwing it as far as you can to Jesus. He catches it.

Short Prayer: "God, this worry is too heavy for me to carry. I am giving it to You. I trust You."

BLOCK 5: PARENT NOTES (The Secret Weapon)

The Doctrine: Sovereignty & Peace Anxiety usually comes from trying to control things we can't control. The doctrine of God's Sovereignty allows us to release control to the One who actually has it.

Why It Matters

- **Mental Health:** Kids today are anxious. They carry the weight of the world on their phones/tablets. We need to teach them they are not the General of the Universe; God is. They can resign from the job of worrying about everything.

Common Misunderstandings to Avoid

- **Misunderstanding:** "If I have faith, I won't feel fear."

  ○ **Correction:** Courage isn't the absence of fear; it's trusting God *in the middle* of fear. David said, "When I am afraid, I will trust in you" (Psalm 56:3). He felt fear, then he chose trust.

Scripts for Hard Questions

- **Q: "Why doesn't God just stop all the bad guys?"**

  - A: "One day, He will! When Jesus comes back, He will fix everything. But right now, He is being patient to give people time to turn to Him. We are living in the 'in-between' time."

Extra Bible Anchors: Philippians 4:6–7; 1 Peter 5:7

Teach-It-Back (30 Seconds) "If you are in a storm, is it better to be the captain of a tiny boat, or a passenger on a giant battleship? (Passenger). Trusting God is letting Him be the Captain."

MEMORY (One-Liner + Catechism Q/A)

One-Line Definition I can trust God when I am afraid because He is bigger than my fears.

Q/A Q: What should we do when we are afraid? **A:** We should trust in God, who is our refuge and strength.

Notes:

WEEK 18: LIFE SKILL: THANKFULNESS & GRATITUDE

BLOCK 1: KID PAGE (Big Idea + Anchor Verse)

Big Idea Gratitude is the superpower that fights envy. Envy is looking at what others have and feeling angry that you don't have it. Gratitude is looking at what God has given *you* and feeling happy. God gives us exactly what we need, when we need it.

Anchor Verse 1 Thessalonians 5:18

In Kid Words "Give thanks in everything; for this is God's will for you in Christ Jesus."

Key Words

- **Envy:** Wanting what someone else has so much that you are unhappy.

- **Contentment:** Being happy with what you have right now.

More Bible places to look: Hebrews 13:5; James 1:17; Psalm 23:1; Philippians 4:11–12

BLOCK 2: STORY PAGE (Real Life Scenario)

Story Title: The Comparison Spiral

Setting: Skate park (or playground).

Problem: Ethan watched his friend, Noah, do a perfect kickflip on his new skateboard. Noah's board was brand new, professional grade. Ethan looked down at his own scratched-up board with the chipped wheels. *Noah gets everything,* Ethan thought. *He's better at skating, he has better stuff, everyone likes him.* A sour feeling filled Ethan's stomach.

Choice Moment: Ethan wanted to say something mean. "Your board color is ugly," popped into his head. He could let the envy win, or he could fight it with gratitude.

Small Resolution: Ethan took a breath. He remembered his dad saying, "Envy is a joy-stealer." He forced a smile. "Nice move, Noah! That board is smooth." As soon as he said it, the sour feeling went away. He looked at his own board. It was old, but it could still roll. "Race you to the bench!" he yelled.

Quick Takeaway: Being happy for others and thankful for what we have keeps our hearts happy.

<u>BLOCK 3: TALK-IT-OUT (Discussion + Coaching)</u>

1. **Understanding:** What was "stealing" Ethan's joy in the story? (Comparing himself to Noah).

2. **Connection:** Why is it hard to say "Good job" when someone else wins or gets something cool?

3. **Application:** Let's try the "Glad Game." Name one thing you are glad you have, and one thing you are glad your friend has.

If your kid says: "But it really IS unfair. They have everything!" **Try:** "It looks that way from the outside. But everyone has hard things, even if we can't see them. And remember, God gives us different gifts. We don't need to look at their plate; we need to enjoy what's on ours."

- **If your kid says:** "I want to be famous/rich." **Try:** "Those things seem cool, but they don't fix our hearts. Only Jesus does that. And He has given you the greatest treasure, Himself!"

<u>BLOCK 4: PRACTICE (One Habit This Week)</u>

The Habit: The "No-Complaining" Challenge

When We'll Do It: For one whole day (pick a day).

What to Watch For: Try to go from breakfast to bedtime without complaining about *anything* (food, weather, siblings). If you slip, say three things you are thankful for to "reset."

Short Prayer: "God, You are a generous Giver. Thank You for all You have given me. Help me not to look over the fence at what others have."

<u>BLOCK 5: PARENT NOTES (The Secret Weapon)</u>

The Doctrine: God's Goodness & Generosity Envy is actually a theological problem. It whispers, "God got it wrong. He gave them too much and me too little." Gratitude affirms, "God is Good, and He knows what is best for me."

Why It Matters

- **Social Media:** We live in the age of comparison. Kids are bombarded with "highlight reels" of others. Gratitude is the only shield strong enough to protect their hearts from constant dissatisfaction.

Common Misunderstandings to Avoid

- **Misunderstanding:** "I'll be grateful when I get what I want."

  ◦ **Correction:** Gratitude is a muscle. If you aren't grateful for what you have now, you won't be grateful when you get more.

- **Misunderstanding:** "God wants me to be poor/miserable."

  ◦ **Correction:** No! God gives us all things to enjoy (1 Timothy 6:17). But He wants us to love the Giver more than the gift.

Scripts for Hard Questions

- **Q: "Why are some people rich and some poor?"**

  ◦ A: "The Bible tells us to work hard and be wise, but it also says God is the one who gives wealth. Sometimes we don't know why God gives more to some. But we know He expects those who have a lot to be generous and help those who have a little."

Extra Bible Anchors: Exodus 20:17 (The 10th Commandment: Do not covet); 1 Timothy 6:6–8

Teach-It-Back (30 Seconds) "If you are eating a yummy ice cream cone, should you enjoy it, or stare at someone else's cone to see if it's bigger? (Enjoy yours!)."

MEMORY (One-Liner + Catechism Q/A)

One-Line Definition Gratitude fights envy by reminding us that God is good to us.

Q/A Q: How do we show we love God? **A:** By believing in His Son Jesus and being thankful for all His gifts.

Notes:

Part 3: Us & What Went Wrong

This is where Christianity stops being "rules" and becomes a **Person**. In this part we focus on **Jesus.** His life, His true humanity and true divinity, His death, and His resurrection.

The goal isn't just that your kids can answer questions about Jesus. The goal is that they begin to **marvel** at Him.. to see Him as the King who is real, present, and worth following with their whole lives.

Each week will keep doing what this book does best: take something big and historic and bring it right to the kitchen table.

The stories help your kids connect Jesus to real fears, real sin, real friendships, and real hope, so faith becomes more than a Sunday word. It becomes the center of the whole map.

WEEK 19: HUMANS IN GOD'S IMAGE

BLOCK 1: KID PAGE (Big Idea + Anchor Verse)

Big Idea God created everything in the world, but He made human beings completely different from the animals. You were made to be like a mirror that reflects what God is like to the rest of the world. Because every person is made in God's image, every single human being, no matter who they are, is valuable and deserves to be treated with dignity.

Anchor Verse Genesis 1:27

In Kid Words God created human beings in His own image. He created them to be like Him; He created them male and female.

Key Words

- **Image of God:** The special status God gave only to humans, making us like Him so we can represent Him on earth.

- **Dignity:** The incredible value and worth someone has just because they exist, not because of what they can do.

- **Reflect:** To show or copy the character of someone else, just like a mirror reflects a face.

More Bible Places to Look Genesis 9:6; Psalm 8:3–8; Psalm 139:14; Colossians 3:10; James 3:9

BLOCK 2: STORY PAGE (Real Life Scenario)

Story Title: The "Funny" Nickname   **Setting:** The school cafeteria during a loud lunch period.

The Problem Sam sat down with his usual group of friends. Across the table, Leo whispered, "Hey, watch this." He pointed at a quiet kid named David, who was sitting alone and eating yogurt. "Hey, *Dairy Queen!*" Leo shouted. The whole table erupted in laughter. It wasn't a clever nickname, but everyone laughed because Leo was the one saying it. Leo looked at Sam, waiting for him to laugh too. "He eats yogurt every day. It fits! Come on, it's funny."

The Choice Sam felt that familiar squeeze in his chest. He could laugh, give Leo a high-five, and stay comfortable in the group. Or, he could stay quiet and risk Leo turning the jokes on him.

The Resolution Sam forced a half-smile but didn't laugh. "I don't know, man," Sam mumbled, looking down at his tray. "Seems kind of mean. He's not bothering anyone." The table went quiet for a second. Leo rolled his eyes and said, "You're no fun," before turning to talk to someone else. It was awkward, and Sam's face felt hot, but he didn't join in.

The Takeaway We don't make fun of people, even when it's "funny," because insulting a person is actually insulting the God who made them.

BLOCK 3: TALK-IT-OUT (Discussion + Coaching)

1. Have you ever heard someone get called a name that was supposed to be a "joke" but felt mean?

2. Why is it so easy to forget that a person we find annoying or different is actually made by God?

3. If you really believed the difficult kid at school was a masterpiece made by God, how would that change the way you talk to them?

If your kid says: "But it was just a joke! We were just having fun." **Try:** "I love that you have a sense of humor. But people aren't just targets for our jokes; they are God's artwork. Do you think we can have fun without tearing apart something God made?"

If your kid says: "But he really is weird/annoying." **Try:** "Sometimes people are hard to get along with. But being annoying doesn't erase the image of God. Even if we don't hang out with them, how can we show them basic respect?"

BLOCK 4: PRACTICE (One Habit This Week)

The Habit: The "Image Check" This week, whenever you see someone who is annoying, difficult, or just different from you, catch yourself and say in your head: *"God made them in His image."*

When we'll do it At school, on the bus, or even when watching videos online.

What to watch for Notice if saying that sentence in your head changes how you feel about them. It's hard to hate someone when you remind yourself they belong to God.

Prayer God, thank You for making us in Your image. Please help me see people the way You see them. When I want to be mean or make fun of someone, remind me that You made them and that they matter to You. Amen.

BLOCK 5: PARENT NOTES (The Secret Weapon)

The Doctrine: The Image of God The doctrine of the "Image of God" (Latin: *Imago Dei*) is the foundation for how we view humanity. It means that human beings are not just advanced animals or biological accidents. We were created specifically to represent God on earth.

Think of it like a **royal statue**. In ancient times, a king would place a statue of himself in a faraway province to say, "This land belongs to me; I rule here." Humans are God's living statues. We are placed here to show the world what God is like, how He rules, creates, loves, and orders things. This gives every human intrinsic dignity. You don't have dignity because you are smart, athletic, or good-looking. You have dignity because you bear the stamp of the King.

Why it matters

- **It kills racism and bullying:** You cannot mistreat a person without mistreating the God who made them (James 3:9).

- **It gives value to everyone:** The unborn, the elderly, the disabled, and the "annoying kid" all have equal value in God's eyes.

- **It defines our purpose:** We aren't here just to consume; we are here to reflect God's goodness to the world.

Common Misunderstandings to Avoid

- **Misunderstanding:** "Being in God's image means we physically look like God."

  - **Correction:** God is Spirit (John 4:24) and does not have a physical body. Being in His image refers to our nature, our ability to reason, love, make moral choices, and rule over creation.

- **Misunderstanding:** "Sin erased the image of God."

  - **Correction:** Sin *damaged* the image (like graffiti on the royal statue), but it did not destroy it. Even people who don't know Jesus are still image-bearers and deserve protection and respect (Genesis 9:6).

How to answer follow-up questions

- **"Does God love bad people?"**

  - "Yes. God doesn't love the bad things they do, but He loves *them* because He made them. That's why He sent Jesus, to wash the 'mud' off His statues so they can shine like Him again."

- **"Why are some people born with disabilities if they are in God's image?"**

  - "Being in God's image isn't about having a perfect body or a high IQ. It's about being a human soul made by God. A person with a disability reflects God's image just as much as an Olympic athlete."

- **"Can I still make fun of my brother?"**

  - "You can have fun *with* your brother, but you can't make fun *of* him. There's a difference between laughing together and laughing at him. He's God's creation, so handle with care."

Extra Bible Anchors for Parents Genesis 1:26–28; Psalm 8; James 3:9–10.

Teach-it-back Prompt (30 Seconds) "Hey, look at that person over there. In your own words, why do they matter to God?" (Answer: Because God made them in His image/like a mirror.)

MEMORY (One-Liner + Catechism Q/A)

One-Liner Every human being is made in God's image and has dignity.

Optional Q/A Q: How are humans different from animals? **A:** God made humans in His own image to represent Him on earth.

Notes:

BLOCK 1: KID PAGE (Big Idea + Anchor Verse)

Big Idea Sin is more than just making a mistake or breaking a rule. Sin is a heart problem where we try to take God's crown and be the king of our own lives. It separates us from God because He is holy and perfect, and sin cannot stay in His presence.

Anchor Verse Romans 3:23

In Kid Words Every single person has sinned and fallen short of God's glorious standard.

Key Words

- **Sin:** Anything we think, say, or do that disobeys God or says, "I don't need You."

- **Holy:** Totally perfect, clean, and set apart from anything bad.

- **Separation:** Being kept apart from someone; sin puts a wall between us and God.

More Bible Places to Look Genesis 3:1–7; Isaiah 53:6; Isaiah 59:2; 1 John 1:8; James 4:17

BLOCK 2: STORY PAGE (Real Life Scenario)

Story Title: The "Forgotten" Chore   **Setting:** The living room, right before screen time.

The Problem Tyler knew the rule: "No video games until the dishwasher is unloaded." But his friends were already online in the lobby, waiting for him. He glanced at the kitchen. The "Clean" light was glowing green on the dishwasher. *It will take too long,* he thought. *Mom is in the backyard; she won't notice until later.* He grabbed the controller and put on his headset. When Mom walked in ten minutes later and asked, "Did you finish the dishes?" Tyler didn't even look up. "Yeah, I think I did it earlier," he mumbled.

The Choice Tyler felt a knot in his stomach. He could pause the game, tell the truth, and take the consequence. Or he could keep playing and hope Mom didn't check the kitchen until he was done.

The Resolution Mom walked to the kitchen and opened the dishwasher. It was full. She turned off the TV. Tyler sighed, "I just... I forgot, okay?" But they both knew he hadn't forgotten. He had chosen what he wanted over what was true. "It's not just about the dishes, Tyler," Mom said quietly. "It's about looking me in the eye and lying to get what you want."

The Takeaway Sin isn't just "forgetting" or making a mistake; it's a choice in our hearts to say, "I care more about what I want than what is right."

BLOCK 3: TALK-IT-OUT (Discussion + Coaching)

1. In the story, was Tyler's sin just about the dishwasher, or was it about something else?

2. Why is it easier to say "I made a mistake" than to say "I sinned"?

3. How does sin feel like a wall between you and your parents (or God)?

If your kid says: "But I didn't mean to!" **Try:** "Sometimes we make accidents, like spilling milk. That's a mistake. But when we choose to hide it or lie about it, that's sin. Do you see the difference?"

If your kid says: "Everyone else lies sometimes." **Try:** "That is true, everyone struggles with sin. That's exactly why we all need Jesus. Just because everyone is sick with sin doesn't mean we don't need a Doctor, right?"

BLOCK 4: PRACTICE (One Habit This Week)

The Habit: The 10-Second Truth This week, if you do something wrong (like hit your sibling or sneak a treat), try to admit it within 10 seconds. Don't hide.

When we'll do it Anytime we mess up or break a rule.

What to watch for Notice how scary it feels right before you tell the truth, but how much lighter you feel after you say it. Hiding makes us feel heavy.

Prayer God, I know I sin. Sometimes I want to be the boss instead of obeying You. Please forgive me. Thank You that I don't have to hide from You. Amen.

BLOCK 5: PARENT NOTES (The Secret Weapon)

The Doctrine: Sin Sin is often trivialized as "bad behavior" or "oopsies." But biblically, sin (Greek: *hamartia*) means "missing the mark." It is a condition of the heart that is hostile to God. It isn't just that we *do* bad things; it's that we *are* bent away from God.

Think of sin like a **heart virus**. It affects everything, our thoughts, our words, and our actions. You can put a bandage on the outside (behavior modification), but that doesn't fix the virus on the inside. We teach our kids about sin not to shame them, but to show them their need for a Savior. If they think they are "basically good people who make mistakes," they won't see why they need the Cross.

Why it matters

- **It explains the mess:** It explains why the world (and our home) is broken. It's not just "bad luck"; it's the result of rebellion.

- **It levels the ground:** Parents and kids are in the same boat. We are all sinners in need of grace. You aren't the perfect judge; you are a fellow sinner helping them.

- **It points to Jesus:** We cannot fix the "heart virus" on our own. We need a new heart.

Common Misunderstandings to Avoid

- **Misunderstanding:** "Sin is just the really bad stuff like stealing or killing."

  - **Correction:** Sin is *any* want of conformity to God's law. Pride, selfishness, and envy are sins just as much as robbery.

- **Misunderstanding:** "If I do good things, it cancels out my sin."

  - **Correction:** Sin is a debt we cannot pay. Doing good chores doesn't erase a lie. Only forgiveness can deal with sin.

How to answer follow-up questions

- **"Did God make sin?"**

  - "No. God made everything good. He gave humans the freedom to choose love or choose themselves. Sin happened when humans used that freedom to choose themselves instead of God."

- **"Why does God punish sin?"**

  - "Because God is good. Imagine a judge who let bad guys go free because he 'wanted to be nice.' He wouldn't be a good judge. God loves the world too much to let evil win."

- **"Am I a bad kid?"**

  - "You are a kid made in God's image who is loved like crazy, but you also have a sinful heart that needs Jesus, just like Mom/Dad does."

Extra Bible Anchors for Parents Romans 3:10–12; Romans 6:23; 1 John 1:8–9.

Teach-it-back Prompt (30 Seconds) "If someone asked you, 'What is sin?', what would you tell them?" (Answer: Choosing my way instead of God's way; missing the mark.)

MEMORY (One-Liner + Catechism Q/A)

One-Liner Sin is rejecting God to be the king of my own life.

Optional Q/A Q: What is sin? **A:** Sin is any want of conformity unto, or transgression of, the law of God.

Notes:

WEEK 21: THE FALL'S EFFECTS

BLOCK 1: KID PAGE (Big Idea + Anchor Verse)

Big Idea When sin entered the world, it broke everything. It didn't just break our relationship with God; it broke our relationships with each other and even nature itself. That is why we have sadness, sickness, and death. The world is not the way it was supposed to be.

Anchor Verse Romans 8:22

In Kid Words We know that the whole creation has been groaning together like it is in pain, right up until now.

Key Words

- **The Fall:** The moment Adam and Eve sinned, and the world broke.

- **Curse:** The consequence of sin that brought pain, hard work, and death into the world.

- **Groaning:** A deep sadness or sound of pain; the Bible says the earth "groans" for God to fix it.

More Bible Places to Look Genesis 3:17–19; Romans 5:12; Revelation 21:4; Psalm 34:18

BLOCK 2: STORY PAGE (Real Life Scenario)

Story Title: The Empty Dog Bed

Setting: The backyard, near the big oak tree.

The Problem Maya stared at the spot under the tree where they had just buried Buster. It felt wrong. The sun was shining, and the birds were singing, but Maya felt like a heavy rock was sitting on her chest. Buster had been her dog since she was a baby. "It's not fair," she whispered. "Why do things have to die? Why couldn't God just fix him?"

The Choice Maya felt angry at everything, at the vet, at the cancer, even at God. She wanted to run to her room and slam the door. She could shut everyone out, or she could let her dad, who was standing quietly beside her, into her sadness.

The Resolution Dad crouched down next to her. He didn't say, "It's okay," because it wasn't. "I hate this too, Maya," he said softly. "Death is awful. It's not how God made the world to be." Maya leaned into him and cried. It didn't bring Buster back, but knowing that the sadness made sense, that the world *was* broken, helped her feel less alone.

The Takeaway It is okay to be sad when sad things happen. Death and sickness are enemies that invaded God's good world, but one day, God promises to defeat them.

BLOCK 3: TALK-IT-OUT (Discussion + Coaching)

1. Why does it feel so "wrong" when someone dies or gets really sick? (Hint: Because we were made for life, not death.)

2. Have you ever seen something broken in the world (like trash in a park, or people fighting) and wished it could be fixed?

3. How does it help to know that God hates death and sadness even more than we do?

If your kid says: "Is my dog in heaven?" **Try:** "The Bible doesn't tell us for sure about animals, but we know God loves His creation even more than we do. We can trust Him to do what is best and beautiful."

If your kid says: "Why didn't God stop it?" **Try:** "That is the hardest question. We know God is strong enough to stop it, but right now, we live in a world broken by sin. He promises that one day He will wipe away every tear, but for now, He cries with us."

BLOCK 4: PRACTICE (One Habit This Week)

The Habit: The "New Creation" Spotter This week, keep your eyes open for things that are "broken" (sadness, fighting, weeds, sickness). When you see them, whisper: *"Come, Lord Jesus."* This is a prayer asking God to hurry up and fix the world.

When we'll do it When we see something sad on the news, get a scrape on the knee, or see an ambulance.

What to watch for Notice that you aren't just sad, you are hopeful. You know the fix is coming.

Prayer Lord, the world is broken. We see it in sickness, fighting, and death. We are sad, but we are not hopeless. Please come back and make everything new again. Amen.

BLOCK 5: PARENT NOTES (The Secret Weapon)

The Doctrine: The Effects of the Fall When Adam and Eve sinned (Genesis 3), the result wasn't just a "time out." It was a cosmic catastrophe. Theologically, we call this "The Fall." It brought three types of death:

1. **Spiritual Death:** Separation from God.

2. **Physical Death:** Bodies eventually fail and die.

3. **Creation's Decay:** Natural disasters, disease, and entropy.

We need to validate our kids' intuition that **death is wrong**. When a child cries over a dead pet or a grandparent, they are responding correctly to the Fall. Don't rush to hush them with platitudes. Affirm that death is an intruder. It wasn't in the Garden of Eden, and it won't be in the New Earth.

Why it matters

- **It validates grief:** Your child isn't wrong for being sad. Grief is the proper response to a broken world.

- **It creates longing:** If the world were perfect now, we wouldn't need Jesus to return. The brokenness makes us groan for redemption (Romans 8).

- **It prevents cynicism:** We can explain bad things without blaming God's character. The world is broken because of sin, not because God is mean.

Common Misunderstandings to Avoid

- **Misunderstanding:** "Death is just a natural part of the circle of life."

  - **Correction:** Biologically, things die. But theologically, death is "the last enemy" (1 Corinthians 15:26). It is unnatural to God's original design.

- **Misunderstanding:** "If bad things happen, God must be mad at me."

  - **Correction:** We live in a fallen world where rain falls on the just and the unjust. A flat tire or a cold doesn't mean God is punishing you personally; it means the world is groaning.

How to answer follow-up questions

- **"Why doesn't God fix it right now?"**

  - "He is waiting so that more people have time to come to know Him before the end. He is being patient (2 Peter 3:9)."

- **"Will we still be sad in heaven?"**

  - "No. The Bible says God will wipe away every tear. There will be no more death or crying or pain (Revelation 21:4)."

- **"Why did God put the tree in the garden if He knew this would happen?"**

  - "God wanted real love, not robot love. Real love requires a choice. He knew we would choose wrong, but He already had a plan to save us, Jesus."

Extra Bible Anchors for Parents Genesis 3:14–19; Romans 8:18–25; Revelation 21:1–5.

Teach-it-back Prompt (30 Seconds) "Why do sad things like sickness and death happen?" (Answer: Because of the Fall/Sin broke the world.)

MEMORY (One-Liner + Catechism Q/A)

One-Liner Sin broke the world, bringing sadness and death, but God promises to make it new.

Optional Q/A Q: What happened to the world after Adam and Eve sinned? **A:** The world became broken, and pain and death entered in.

Notes:

WEEK 22: COVENANT & PROMISE

BLOCK 1: KID PAGE (Big Idea + Anchor Verse)

Big Idea A "covenant" is a very serious promise that binds two people together. In the Bible, God makes covenants with His people. He says, "I will be your God, and you will be My people." Even when we fail or don't understand His rules, God keeps His covenant promises forever.

Anchor Verse Genesis 17:7

In Kid Words I will keep my special promise between Me and you and your children after you. It is a promise that lasts forever: I will be your God.

Key Words

- **Covenant:** A binding agreement or promise between two parties (much stronger than a contract).

- **Faithful:** Keeping your word, no matter what happens.

- **Promise:** Giving your word that you will do something.

More Bible Places to Look Exodus 19:5; Jeremiah 31:33; Hebrews 8:10; 2 Timothy 2:13

BLOCK 2: STORY PAGE (Real Life Scenario)

Story Title: The "Unfair" No   **Setting:** The kitchen table on a Saturday morning.

The Problem "But everyone else is going!" Lucas pleaded. His friends were going to a movie that Lucas wasn't allowed to see. "I know it feels huge right now," Dad said calmly, "but the answer is no. That movie has stuff in it that isn't good for your heart." Lucas crossed his arms. "You just don't want me to have fun. If you loved me, you'd let me go." He felt like the relationship was broken. How could Dad be *for* him and still say "no"?

The Choice Lucas wanted to yell, "I hate you!" and storm off. He felt like Dad was the enemy. But he looked at Dad's face. Dad wasn't angry; he looked steady. Lucas had to decide: *Is* Dad trying to ruin my life, or is he keeping a *promise to take care of me?*

The Resolution Lucas huffed and pushed away from the table. He didn't totally get it. But later, when Dad came in to shoot hoops, Lucas went out. "I'm still mad," Lucas said. "I know," Dad replied, passing him the ball. "And I'm still your dad. I'm not going anywhere." Lucas realized the "No" didn't break the relationship. Dad was committed to him, even when they di sagreed.

The Takeaway A covenant means God is committed to being our Father even when we are confused, angry, or don't understand His rules.

BLOCK 3: TALK-IT-OUT (Discussion + Coaching)

1. Why did Lucas think his dad didn't love him? (Because he didn't get his way.)

2. What is the difference between a "contract" (I do this if you do that) and a "covenant" (I am committed to you no matter what)?

3. How does it make you feel to know God has made a covenant to be your God forever?

If your kid says: "But if I disobey, won't God leave me?" **Try:** "That's the amazing thing about God's covenant. He is faithful even when we are faithless. If you are His child, your sin might make Him sad, but it won't make Him leave."

If your kid says: "Promises are easy to break." **Try:** "Human promises are breakable. But God is not like us. He cannot lie. When He makes a covenant, He stakes His whole reputation on keeping it."

BLOCK 4: PRACTICE (One Habit This Week)

The Habit: The "Whatever Happens" Promise Think of one thing you can promise to do for a family member this week *no matter what* (e.g., helping a sibling clean up, reading a book together).

When we'll do it Pick a specific time (like Tuesday night).

What to watch for Notice if you feel like breaking the promise when you get tired or annoyed. Do it anyway. That is a tiny picture of covenant love.

Prayer God, thank You for being a Covenant-keeping God. Thank You that You never break Your promises to us. Help me to trust You even when I don't understand Your "no." Amen.

BLOCK 5: PARENT NOTES (The Secret Weapon)

The Doctrine: Covenant The Bible is organized around covenants (Noahic, Abrahamic, Mosaic, Davidic, New Covenant). A covenant is different from a contract.

- **Contract:** "I will do X if you do Y." (Based on performance; easy to break).

- **Covenant:** "I give myself to you." (Based on relationship; binding).

When God enters a covenant, He binds Himself to His people. He says, "I will be their God." This gives us security. We aren't worried that God will fire us if we have a bad week. The New Covenant in Jesus is the ultimate promise, it relies on *Jesus's* performance, not ours.

Why it matters

- **Security:** Kids need to know the floor won't drop out. God's love is covenantal, it's fixed.

- **Context for Rules:** God's laws (Commandments) come *after* the Covenant relationship. He saves Israel from Egypt (Covenant grace) *then* gives the law. Obedience is a response to love, not a way to earn it.

- **Hope:** When we fail (and we will), the Covenant stands because God stands.

Common Misunderstandings to Avoid

- **Misunderstanding:** "The Old Testament is about law, and the New Testament is about grace."

  - **Correction:** God made gracious covenants in the OT too (like with Abraham). He has always been a God of promise.

- **Misunderstanding:** "If I sin too much, God breaks the covenant."

  - **Correction:** In the New Covenant, Jesus took the penalty for our covenant-breaking. Our security depends on Him, not our perfect record.

How to answer follow-up questions

- **"Does God make covenants with us today?"**

  - "Yes! Through Jesus, we enter into the 'New Covenant.' When we trust Jesus, God promises to forgive our sins and write His law on our hearts."

- **"Is marriage a covenant?"**

  - "Yes. That's why Mom and Dad promised to stay together 'for better or worse.' It's a picture of how God loves His people."

- **"What if I break a promise to God?"**

  - "God expects us to be honest, but He knows we are weak. When you break a promise, tell Him you're sorry. He will never break His promise to forgive you."

Extra Bible Anchors for Parents Genesis 15 (God walks through the pieces); Jeremiah 31:31–34; Luke 22:20.

Teach-it-back Prompt (30 Seconds) "What is the difference between a contract and a covenant?" (Answer: A contract is about a deal; a covenant is about a relationship/promise that lasts.)

<u>MEMORY (One-Liner + Catechism Q/A)</u>

One-Liner A covenant is God's unbreakable promise to be our God and make us His people.

Optional Q/A Q: How can we trust God? **A:** We can trust God because He is faithful and always keeps His covenant promises.

<u>Notes:</u>

WEEK 23: GRACE

BLOCK 1: KID PAGE (Big Idea + Anchor Verse)

Big Idea Grace is getting a gift you do not deserve. We call it "unmerited favor." We all deserve punishment because of our sin, but God chooses to give us love, forgiveness, and life instead. You cannot earn grace; you can only say "thank you" and receive it.

Anchor Verse Ephesians 2:8

In Kid Words You have been saved by grace through faith. It is not something you did to earn it; it is a gift from God.

Key Words

- **Grace:** Being given something good (like forgiveness) when you deserved something bad (punishment).

- **Mercy:** Not getting the punishment you *do* deserve.

- **Gift:** Something free that you don't work for.

More Bible Places to Look Romans 3:24; Titus 3:5; Romans 11:6; 2 Corinthians 12:9

BLOCK 2: STORY PAGE (Real Life Scenario)

Story Title: The Library Book Disaster

Setting: The school library, near the return desk.

The Problem Mia's stomach hurt. In her backpack was a library book that was not just overdue, it was ruined. Her juice box had exploded on it. The pages were purple and sticky. She knew the rule: if you ruin a book, you pay for it and you lose checkout privileges. She walked up to the librarian, Mrs. Higgins, who was known for being strict.

The Choice Mia could lie and say she found it that way, or she could own up. With shaky hands, she pulled out the purple, soggy mess. "I'm so sorry," Mia whispered, tearing up. "I ruined it. I don't have the money to pay for it yet." She braced herself for the scolding.

The Resolution Mrs. Higgins looked at the book, then at Mia's terrified face. She sighed, but then her face softened. She took the book and dropped it in the trash. Then she typed something on her computer. "I'm wiping the fine, Mia," she said. "And you can check out a new book today." Mia blinked. "But... why? I ruined it." "Because I know you're sorry," Mrs. Higgins said. "And today, I'm choosing to be kind."

The Takeaway Mia walked out with a new book she didn't pay for and a relief she didn't earn. That is a tiny picture of grace.

BLOCK 3: TALK-IT-OUT (Discussion + Coaching)

1. Why was Mia surprised by what Mrs. Higgins did?

2. If Mia had paid for the book with her own money, would that have been grace? (No, that would be paying a debt.)

3. God gives us grace. What is the "purple soggy book" (sin) that we bring to Him?

If your kid says: "That's not fair! She should have been punished." **Try:** "You are right. It wasn't fair. Grace isn't fair. If God were 'fair' with us, we would all be in trouble. Grace is better than fair."

If your kid says: "I have to be good so God will love me." **Try:** "God loves you because He is good, not because you are good. You obey Him *because* He loved you first, not to *make* Him love you."

BLOCK 4: PRACTICE (One Habit This Week)

The Habit: The Grace Pass This week, if someone in your family makes a mistake (spills something, forgets a chore, annoys you), give them a "Grace Pass." Say, "I forgive you," and help them fix it without complaining.

When we'll do it When a sibling or parent messes up.

What to watch for It is hard to give grace! It feels better to stay mad. But giving grace reminds us of how much grace God gives us.

Prayer Jesus, thank You for grace. I know I mess up a lot, but You always love me and forgive me. Help me to give that same grace to my family today. Amen.

BLOCK 5: PARENT NOTES (The Secret Weapon)

The Doctrine: Grace Grace is the heart of the Christian faith. Every other religion is about humans working their way up to God (karma, obeying rules, being good). Christianity is God coming down to us.

- **Justice:** Getting what you deserve.

- **Mercy:** Not getting what you deserve (punishment).

- **Grace:** Getting what you don't deserve (favor, adoption, heaven).

Think of grace like a **birthday gift**. If you have to mow the lawn to get the gift, it's not a gift; it's a wage (Romans 4:4). Grace must be free, or it isn't grace.

Why it matters

- **It kills pride:** We can't brag about being Christians because we didn't earn it. We are beggars who found bread.

- **It motivates obedience:** When you realize how much God has done for you, you *want* to obey Him. Guilt is a bad fuel for obedience; gratitude is rocket fuel.

- **It creates safety:** Your kids need to know that your home is a place of grace. High standards? Yes. But plenty of forgiveness when they fall.

Common Misunderstandings to Avoid

- **Misunderstanding:** "Grace means it doesn't matter if I sin."

  - **Correction:** That is called "cheap grace." Real grace cost Jesus His life. When we understand the cost, we don't want to keep sinning (Romans 6:1-2).

- **Misunderstanding:** "I have to do my part, and God does His part."

  - **Correction:** In salvation, we bring the sin; God brings the grace. We contribute nothing to our salvation except the sin that made it necessary.

How to answer follow-up questions

- **"Is** God **nice to everyone?"**

  - "God shows 'common grace' to everyone, sunshine, food, life. But He shows 'saving grace' to those who trust in Jesus."

- **"Why** is grace hard **to accept?"**

  - "Because we like to be in control. We like to think, 'I did this!' Accepting grace means admitting we are helpless."

- **"Can I earn more grace?"**

  - "No. The tank is full. God cannot love you more than He does right now in Jesus."

Extra Bible Anchors **for Parents** Romans 11:6; Ephesians 1:7; 2 Timothy 1:9.

Teach-it-back Prompt (30 Seconds) "If grace is a gift, what happens if you try to pay for it?" (Answer: It stops being a gift and becomes a payment. Grace is free.)

MEMORY (One-Liner + Catechism Q/A)

One-Liner Grace is God giving us the forgiveness and love we could never earn.

Optional Q/A Q: What is grace? **A:** Grace is God's kindness to us when we deserved punishment.

Notes:

WEEK 24: REVIEW (WHAT WENT WRONG)

BLOCK 1: KID PAGE (Big Idea + Anchor Verse)

Big Idea We have learned a lot! God made humans in His image (like mirrors). But we sinned (the heart virus) and broke the world (The Fall). But God didn't leave us broken. He made a Covenant (promise) and showed us Grace (a gift we don't deserve). The story isn't over, God is on a rescue mission.

Anchor Verse Psalm 145:8

In Kid Words The Lord is gracious and full of mercy. He is slow to get angry, and He is overflowing with faithful love.

Key Words

- **Review:** Looking back at what we learned so it sticks in our brains.

- **Rescue:** Saving someone who cannot save themselves.

- **Image Bearer:** That's you! Someone made to reflect God.

More Bible Places to Look Review these favorites: Genesis 1:27; Romans 3:23; Ephesians 2:8.

BLOCK 2: STORY PAGE (Real Life Scenario)

Story Title: The Broken Controller Mystery   **Setting:** The family den.

The Problem Dad walked in holding his favorite gaming controller. The joystick was snapped clean off. "Does anyone know what happened to this?" he asked. Sam and his sister, Lily, looked at each other. Sam had stepped on it by accident while chasing Lily, but Lily had left it on the floor. "Lily left it out!" Sam said quickly. "Sam stepped on it!" Lily shouted back.

The Choice They were doing the "Blame Game." (Just like Adam and Eve did in the garden!) They could keep pointing fingers, or someone could stop the cycle.

The Resolution Dad held up a hand. "I see. It sounds like there is plenty of blame to go around. Who is going to own their part?" Sam looked at the broken plastic. He remembered what they talked about this month, sin and taking responsibility. "I stepped on it," Sam said quietly. "I wasn't looking. I'm sorry, Dad." Dad nodded. "Thank you for the truth. The controller is broken, but I'm glad our trust isn't."

The Takeaway When things go wrong, our sinful hearts want to blame others. Grace helps us say, "It was me. I need help."

BLOCK 3: TALK-IT-OUT (Discussion + Coaching)

1. Why did Sam blame Lily first? (Because he was scared/sinful heart).

2. Can you remember the 3 Big Words we learned this month? (Image, Sin, Grace). Which one did Sam show at the end?

3. How does knowing God gives grace help us tell the truth when we break something?

If your kid says: "I don't remember any of the words." **Try:** "That's okay! That's why we review. Let's match them. Which word means 'broken world'? (The Fall/Sin). Which word means 'free gift'? (Grace)."

If your kid says: "Sam should still get in trouble." **Try:** "Consequences are real. He might have to do extra chores to help fix it. But grace means Dad isn't angry at *him* anymore. Relationship restored."

BLOCK 4: PRACTICE (One Habit This Week)

The Habit: The "Help **Me**" Prayer This week, we are practicing being weak so God can be strong. Once a day, find something you can't do on your own (homework, reaching a high shelf, controlling your temper) and ask God (or a parent) for help.

When we'll do it Whenever we feel stuck or frustrated.

What to watch for Sin makes us want to do it all ourselves. Asking for help is a way to kill our pride.

Prayer God, thank You for not quitting on us when we sinned. Thank You for Your covenant and Your grace. I am glad I am Your image-bearer. Help me reflect You this week. Amen.

BLOCK 5: PARENT NOTES (The Secret Weapon)

The Doctrine: Reviewing the **Arc** This week is a "breather." We aren't adding new info; we are cementing the narrative arc.

1. **Creation:** We were made good (Image of God).

2. **Fall:** We messed it up (Sin/Fall).

3. **Redemption (Started):** God promised to fix it (Covenant/Grace).

Review weeks are critical because kids learn by repetition. If they can articulate the problem (Sin) and the solution (Grace), they are building a theological worldview.

Why it matters

- **Connecting the dots:** We don't want kids to have a bag of random Bible facts. We want them to see the Story.

- **Checking the heart:** Is this landing? Do they understand they are sinners? Do they understand grace is free?

- **Building vocabulary:** Being able to use words like "Grace" and "Image of God" gives them tools to process their world.

Common Misunderstandings to Avoid

- **Misunderstanding:** "We are done learning about sin."

  - **Correction:** We never "graduate" from the gospel. We will struggle with sin and need grace until we die.

- **Misunderstanding:** "Review is boring."

  - **Correction:** Repetition is how we master things (like sports or music). Make it a game. Who can define "Grace" the fastest?

How to answer follow-up questions

- **"Why** did God make us if He **knew we would break everything?"**

  - "Because He knew the rescue mission would show His glory even more than the original creation. He loves to save."

- **"How do I know if I have grace?"**

  - "Do you trust Jesus? Do you know you can't save yourself? That trust is the evidence of grace in your heart."

Extra Bible Anchors for Parents Psalm 103 (The Great Psalm of Grace); Ephesians 2:1–10.

Teach-it-back Prompt (30 Seconds) "Let's play 'Word Association.' I say a word, you say the meaning. Me: 'Image of God.' You: (Mirror!) Me: 'Grace.' You: (Gift!)"

MEMORY (One-Liner + Catechism Q/A)

One-Liner We broke God's world with our sin, but God is fixing it with His grace.

Optional Q/A Q: Did God leave us in our sin? **A:** No, but out of His mere good pleasure, He entered into a covenant of grace to deliver us.

Notes:

WEEK 25: LIFE SKILL: CONFESSION & FORGIVENESS

BLOCK 1: KID PAGE (Big Idea + Anchor Verse)

Big Idea Confession means "agreeing with God." When we sin, we don't hide it. We admit it to God and the person we hurt. Forgiveness means letting go of our anger when someone hurts us. These two skills act like soap and water, they keep our relationships clean.

Anchor Verse 1 John 1:9

In Kid Words If we confess our sins, God is faithful and righteous to forgive us our sins and to clean us from all unrighteousness.

Key Words

- **Confess:** To admit what you did wrong and agree that it was sin.

- **Forgive:** To choose to let go of anger and not pay someone back for hurting you.

- **Resentment:** Holding onto anger like a hot coal in your hand.

More Bible Places to Look James 5:16; Proverbs 28:13; Matthew 6:14–15; Ephesians 4:32

BLOCK 2: STORY PAGE (Real Life Scenario)

Story Title: The Stolen Credit   **Setting:** The family kitchen, looking at a school project.

The Problem Ethan and his younger brother, Noah, had built a huge Lego castle together. But when Mom walked in, Noah shouted, "Look what I built, Mom!" Mom clapped. "Wow, Noah! That is amazing!" Noah beamed and didn't mention Ethan at all. Ethan felt his face get hot. *I did the hard parts!* he thought. *He is stealing my credit!*

The Choice Ethan wanted to smash the castle. He wanted to scream, "He's a liar!" and embarrass Noah. Resentment was bubbling up like a volcano.

The Resolution Ethan took a deep breath. He didn't smash the castle. But he did speak up later, calmly. "Noah, it hurt my feelings when you said *you* built it. We built it together." Noah looked down. "I know. I just wanted Mom to be proud. I'm sorry." Ethan had to decide: hold onto the anger or let it go. "It's okay," Ethan said. "Next time, tell her we did it as a team."

The Takeaway When we are hurt, we speak the truth and then forgive. Revenge breaks things; forgiveness fixes them.

BLOCK 3: TALK-IT-OUT (Discussion + Coaching)

1. Why is it so hard to forgive when someone takes credit for your work?

2. What does "confession" feel like? (Scary at first, but good after).

3. Why do we need to confess to God *and* to the person we hurt?

If your kid says: "I will forgive him, but I won't play with him anymore." **Try:** "Forgiveness doesn't mean you have to trust someone instantly if they keep being mean. But it does mean you stop wanting to punish them. Let's start there."

If your kid says: "I didn't do anything wrong! He started it." **Try:** "Even if he started it, did you react with kindness or did you sin back? We are only responsible for *our* sin. Let's confess your part."

BLOCK 4: PRACTICE (One Habit This Week)

The Habit: The Clean Slate Every night before bed, ask yourself: "Is there anyone I am mad at? Is there anyone I need to say sorry to?" Try to go to sleep with a "clean slate" (no anger, no secrets).

When we'll do it Right before prayers at bedtime.

What to watch for Sleeping is easier when you aren't holding a grudge!

Prayer Father, thank You for forgiving me. Please help me to admit when I am wrong. And help me to forgive others just like You forgave me. I don't want to hold onto anger. Amen.

BLOCK 5: PARENT NOTES (The Secret Weapon)

The Doctrine: Confession & Forgiveness This is the practical machinery of the Christian life. Martin Luther said the Christian life is one of "daily repentance."

- **Confession:** It is not telling God something He doesn't know. It is *homologeo* (Greek), "saying the same thing." We agree with God that our action was sin.

- **Forgiveness:** It is cancelling a debt. When we forgive, we absorb the cost of the hurt instead of making the other person pay.

Why it matters

- **Relational Health:** A family that doesn't confess and forgive will eventually stop talking to each other. Resentment builds walls.

- **Modeling:** If you (parent) never say "I'm sorry" to your kids, they will learn that being an adult means pretending you are perfect.

- **Gospel Rehearsal:** Every time we forgive, we act out the gospel.

Common Misunderstandings to Avoid

- **Misunderstanding:** "Forgiving means saying what they did didn't matter."

  - **Correction:** No. Forgiveness admits it *did* matter and it *was* wrong, but chooses to release the debt anyway.

- **Misunderstanding:** "I have to feel happy to forgive."

  - **Correction:** Forgiveness is a choice, not a feeling. You can forgive while still feeling sad or hurt. The feelings often heal later.

How to answer follow-up questions

- **"Why do I have to say sorry to God if He already forgave me?"**

  - "Imagine you broke a window. Dad still loves you (relationship), but you need to talk about it to restore the closeness (fellowship). Confession restores the closeness."

- **"What if they aren't sorry?"**

  - "You can still forgive them in your heart so bitterness doesn't eat you up. But the relationship might not be fixed until they apologize."

- **"How many times do I have to forgive?"**

  - "Jesus said 70 times 7 (Matthew 18:22). That means... don't count. Just keep forgiving."

Extra Bible Anchors for Parents Psalm 32 (The joy of confession); Matthew 18:21–35 (The Unforgiving Servant).

Teach-it-back Prompt (30 Seconds) "What acts like soap and water for our friendships?" (Answer: Confession and Forgiveness.)

<u>MEMORY (One-Liner + Catechism Q/A)</u>

One-Liner Confession is admitting my sin; forgiveness is letting go of my anger.

Optional Q/A Q: What should we do when we sin? **A:** We should confess our sins to God and turn away from them.

<u>Notes:</u>

WEEK 26: LIFE SKILL: IDENTITY

BLOCK 1: KID PAGE (Big Idea + Anchor Verse)

Big Idea "Identity" answers the question: *Who am I?* The world says you are what you *do* (your grades, your sports, your likes). But the Bible says you are who God *says* you are. You are His child, loved and chosen. Your performance doesn't change your identity.

Anchor Verse 1 John 3:1

In Kid Words Look at how great a love the Father has given to us, that we should be called God's children. And that is what we are!

Key Words

- **Identity:** Who you truly are.

- **Performance:** How well you do something (winning, getting A's).

- **Accepted:** Being welcomed and loved just as you are.

More Bible Places to Look Psalm 139:13–14; Galatians 3:26; Ephesians 1:5; 1 Peter 2:9

BLOCK 2: STORY PAGE (Real Life Scenario)

Story Title: The Reading Circle   **Setting:** Classroom, reading time.

The Problem It was Chloe's turn to read out loud. Her hands started to sweat. She hated this. She stumbled over the word "determined," saying "de-ter-m... mind." A kid in the back snickered. Chloe's face turned bright red. She felt stupid. The thought hit her hard: *I am the dumbest kid in this class.*

The Choice Chloe wanted to pretend she was sick and go to the nurse. She wanted to hide. She felt like her value was dropping with every mistake she made.

The Resolution Later, at home, Chloe told her mom. "I'm just not smart like the other kids." Mom stopped chopping vegetables. "Chloe, being a fast reader is a skill. It's not who you *are*. You are kind, creative, and a child of God. Reading is just something you're learning. It doesn't define you." Chloe took a breath. She was still a slow reader, but she wasn't a "dumb person." There was a difference.

The Takeaway What you can do (your skills) is not the same as who you are (your identity). You are loved by God even on your worst day.

BLOCK 3: TALK-IT-OUT (Discussion + Coaching)

1. Why did Chloe feel like she was "dumb" just because she stumbled on a word?

2. Fill in the blank: "The world says I am special if I _________. God says I am special because _________."

3. If you failed a big test tomorrow, would God love you any less? Why?

If your kid say: "But I want to be good at things!" **Try:** "Of course! It is good to work hard and learn. But if you fail, you are still YOU. You are a loved kid who missed a goal, not a failure of a person."

If your kid says: "People like the winners best." **Try:** "Sometimes people are shallow. They only look at the outside. But God looks at the heart. And the people who really love you (like us!) love you whether you win or lose."

BLOCK 4: PRACTICE (One Habit This Week)

The Habit: The Name Tag Imagine you are wearing a sticky name tag that says "Child of God." Before you walk into school or practice, tap your chest and remind yourself: "That is my real name."

When we'll do it In the car or at the door before leaving the house.

What to watch for When you know who you are, you don't have to be so scared of making mistakes.

Prayer God, thank You that I don't have to earn Your love. You love me because I am Yours. When I feel like a failure, remind me that I am Your child. Amen.

BLOCK 5: PARENT NOTES (The Secret Weapon)

The Doctrine: Identity in Christ Identity is the crisis of our age. Kids are told they must curate an identity through social media, gender expression, or achievements. This is a crushing burden. The Gospel offers a "received identity." We don't achieve it; we receive it.

- **Justification:** God declares us righteous (not because we are, but because Jesus is).

- **Adoption:** God signs the papers and brings us into the family.

Think of identity like a **Label Maker**. The world tries to stick labels on us: "Smart," "Slow," "Pretty," "Weird." But God puts the ultimate label on us: "MINE." That label is superglue; it doesn't peel off.

Why it matters

- **Resilience:** A kid who knows their identity is in Christ can survive being cut from the team or failing a test. Their foundation is deeper than their circumstances.

- **Humility:** If my worth is a gift from God, I can't look down on others.

- **Peace:** I don't have to "perform" to keep my status.

Common Misunderstandings to Avoid

- **Misunderstanding:** "Identity means I'm perfect."

  - **Correction:** No, it means I am *loved* while being imperfect.

- **Misunderstanding:** "My feelings define my identity."

  - **Correction:** Feelings change like the weather. Identity is like the solid ground. You are God's child even when you feel lonely or sad.

How to answer follow-up questions

- **"What if I mess up really bad?"**

  - "You cannot sin your way out of God's family. You can grieve His heart, but you are still His child."

- **"Why do I care so much what my friends think?"**

  - "Because we were made for connection. It's normal to want friends to like you. But their opinion is just an opinion. God's opinion is the Truth."

Extra Bible Anchors for Parents Galatians 4:4–7; Romans 8:14–17; 1 John 3:1–2.

Teach-it-back Prompt (30 **Seconds)** "Finish this sentence: My grades tell me how I did in school, but they don't tell me __________." (Answer: Who I am / My worth.)

MEMORY (One-Liner + Catechism Q/A)

One-Liner My identity is not what I do; it is who God says I am.

Optional Q/A Q: Who are you? **A:** I am a child of God, loved and chosen by Him.

Notes:

WEEK 27: ADVENT / WAITING ON GOD

BLOCK 1: KID PAGE (Big Idea + Anchor Verse)

Big Idea Advent means "coming." It is the season leading up to Christmas where we practice *waiting*. For thousands of years, God's people waited for the Savior to come and fix the broken world. Now, we celebrate that Jesus came, but we also wait for Him to come back again. Waiting is hard, but God is always on time.

Anchor Verse Isaiah 9:6

In Kid Words A child will be born for us, a son will be given to us. He will be called Wonderful Counselor, Mighty God, Eternal Father, Prince of Peace.

Key Words

- **Advent:** The arrival or "coming" of someone important.

- **Messiah:** The Rescuer God promised to send.

- **Hope:** Trusting that God will do something good in the future, even if we can't see it yet.

More Bible Places to Look Luke 2:25–32 (Simeon waiting); Micah 5:2; Matthew 1:21–23.

BLOCK 2: STORY PAGE (Real Life Scenario)

Story Title: The Longest Month

Setting: The living room, looking at the calendar.

The Problem Jaden wanted the new "Speed-Racer" bike more than anything. Dad had hinted that a big surprise was coming for his birthday, but his birthday was still three weeks away. Every day felt like a year. "Can't I just have it now?" Jaden groaned. "Waiting is the worst." "If I gave it to you now," Mom said, "it wouldn't be ready. Dad is still fixing the brakes in the garage."

The Choice Jaden could mope and complain every day, making himself miserable. Or he could trust that his dad was preparing something great and get excited about the *promise* of the bike.

The Resolution Jaden sighed and circled the date on the calendar. "Okay. I'll wait." When the day finally came, the bike was perfect. It was painted his favorite color, and the brakes were tight. Dad had used the waiting time to make it exactly right. Jaden realized the wait made the gift feel even bigger.

The Takeaway God's people waited centuries for Jesus. Waiting is hard work, but God never forgets His promises. He is preparing something good.

BLOCK 3: TALK-IT-OUT (Discussion + Coaching)

1. What is the hardest thing you have ever had to wait for?

2. Imagine waiting 400 years for a promise! Why do you think God made His people wait so long for Jesus?

3. How is "hoping" different from "wishing"? (Wishing is "maybe"; Hope is "for sure, just not yet.")

If your kid says: "I hate waiting!" **Try:** "Me too! But waiting stretches our 'trust muscles.' It reminds us that we aren't in charge of the timing, God is."

If your kid says: "Is Jesus ever coming back?" **Try:** "Yes. Just like He came the first time exactly when God planned, He will come the second time. We are in the 'Advent' of His second coming right now."

BLOCK 4: PRACTICE (One Habit This Week)

The Habit: The Slow Unwrap (Do this with a small treat or snack). Place a treat in front of you. Set a timer for 2 minutes. Sit and look at it. Thank God for it. Think about how good it will taste. When the timer beeps, eat it!

When we'll do it Once this week before a snack.

What to watch for Did the treat taste better because you had to wait for it? Waiting builds anticipation.

Prayer God, thank You that You always keep Your promises. Thank You for sending Jesus. Help us to wait with patience for You to move in our lives. We trust Your timing. Amen.

BLOCK 5: PARENT NOTES (The Secret Weapon)

The Doctrine: Advent & Eschatology Advent isn't just a countdown to Christmas presents. It is a theological rehearsal of **longing**. The Old Testament saints lived in a state of "not yet." They had the promise (Genesis 3:15), but not the fulfillment. We live in a similar state. We look *back* at the First Advent (Incarnation) with gratitude, and we look *forward* to the Second Advent (Consummation) with hope.

Think of Advent like **Christmas Eve**. You know the gifts are there. You know the celebration is coming. But it isn't morning yet. You have to wait in the dark, trusting the sun will rise.

Why it matters

- **Counter-Culture:** Our culture demands instant gratification (Prime delivery, streaming). Advent teaches the spiritual discipline of patience.

- **Handling Darkness:** Advent acknowledges that the world is dark and needs a Light. It allows us to be honest about pain while holding onto hope.

- **Focus:** It shifts the focus from "What am I getting?" to "Who is coming?"

Common Misunderstandings to Avoid

- **Misunderstanding:** "Advent is just the chocolate calendar."

  - **Correction:** That's a fun tool, but real Advent is a posture of the heart saying, "Come, Lord Jesus."

- **Misunderstanding:** "God is slow."

  - **Correction:** God is never late. Galatians 4:4 says Jesus came "when the fullness of time had come." His timing is precise.

How to answer follow-up questions

- **"Why did God send a baby instead of a soldier?"**

  - "Because He didn't come to fight a war with swords; He came to fight a war with sin. He had to become one of us to save us."

- **"What are we waiting for now?"**

  - "We are waiting for Jesus to return and fix the world completely, no more sickness, no more dying."

- **"Why is the world still broken if Jesus came?"**

  - "He started the rescue mission (D-Day), but the war isn't fully over yet (V-Day). We are living in the time between the victory and the final party."

Extra Bible Anchors for Parents Isaiah 9:2–7; Luke 2:1–20; Romans 8:22–25.

Teach-it-back Prompt (30 Seconds) "What does the word 'Advent' mean?" (Answer: Coming / Arrival.)

MEMORY (One-Liner + Catechism Q/A)

One-Liner Advent is waiting with hope for God to keep His promise.

Optional Q/A Q: Who is the Redeemer of God's people? A: The only Redeemer is the Lord Jesus Christ.

Notes:

Part 4: Jesus

Here's where the gospel gets personal. In this section we'll talk about **sin, grace, forgiveness, adoption, and union with Christ...** and we'll do it in a way that directly speaks to the pressure kids feel to perform, impress, and prove themselves.

The world tells them, "You are what you achieve." Jesus tells them, "You are Mine."

That difference changes everything.

Week by week, your child will learn to name shame, fight lies, and breathe again.

This part is designed to put steel in their spine: **freedom from shame and performance anxiety**, not because they become stronger, but because they learn to rest in what Christ has done and who He says they are.

WEEK 28: JESUS: FULLY GOD & FULLY HUMAN

BLOCK 1: KID PAGE (Big Idea + Anchor Verse)

Big Idea Jesus is not half-God and half-human; He is fully God and fully human at the same time. This matters because as a human, He understands our weakness, sadness, and tiredness perfectly. As God, He has the power to save us, forgive us, and rule over everything.

Anchor Verse Hebrews 4:15

In kid words We have a High Priest who isn't shocked by our weakness because He was tempted just like us, but He never sinned.

Key Words

- **Incarnation:** The moment God the Son became a human being (Jesus) while staying God. It means "taking on flesh."

- **Human:** Jesus had a real body, got hungry, felt sad, and could die.

- **Divine:** Jesus is God. He has all of God's power and character.

More Bible places to look John 1:14; Colossians 2:9; Philippians 2:6–7; Luke 2:52; Matthew 8:24; Mark 4:38; John 11:35

BLOCK 2: STORY PAGE (Real Life Scenario)

Title: Panic at Practice

Setting: A hot soccer field during a tryout for the travel team.

The Problem: Maya was out of breath. The coach was yelling drills, and everyone else seemed faster and stronger. Her legs felt like jelly, and her chest was tight with panic. *I can't do this,* she thought. *I'm too weak. No one understands how hard this is.* She wanted to quit right there and hide in the car.

The Choice Moment: She could fake an injury to get out of it, or she could keep going, even though she felt weak. Just then, she remembered her dad telling her, "Jesus knows what it's like to be tired." It seemed weird to think about God being out of breath, but if Jesus was really human, maybe He *did* get it.

Small Resolution: Maya didn't make the top squad that day, but she didn't quit. She finished the drill. In the car, she told her mom, "I felt so weak." "I know," Mom said. "It's okay to be human. Jesus got tired too. He isn't disappointed in you for being tired; He gets it."

Quick Takeaway: Because Jesus became human, we never have to explain our weakness to a God who doesn't understand.

BLOCK 3: TALK-IT-OUT (Discussion + Coaching)

1. **Understanding:** Why did it help Maya to remember that Jesus gets tired too?

2. **Connection:** When was the last time you felt really weak, tired, or sad? Do you think Jesus understands that feeling?

3. **Application:** If Jesus understands us perfectly, how does that change the way we pray when we are having a bad day?

If your kid says: "If Jesus was God, did He cheat at being human? Like, did He use superpowers to not feel pain?" **Try:** "That's a great question. The Bible says He was *fully* human. He didn't use His God-power to escape the hard parts of being human. He really felt hunger, sadness, and pain, just like we do."

If your kid says: "Why did He have to be human to save us?" **Try:** "To pay for the sins of humans, the Rescuer had to *be* a human. A substitute has to match the person they are replacing. But to survive paying that price, He had to be God."

If your kid says: "Does Jesus know what it's like to play video games or deal with internet bullies?" **Try:** "He didn't have the internet, but He definitely knew what it was like to be teased, misunderstood, and attacked with words. He understands th e *feeling* of those things perfectly."

BLOCK 4: PRACTICE (One Habit This Week)

The Habit: The "He Gets It" Pause When you feel something hard this week (tired, hungry, sad, left out), pause and say: "Jesus, You know what this feels like."

When we'll do it: Right in the moment, at school, practice, or before bed.

What to watch for: Notice if it makes you feel less lonely to know God understands exactly how you feel.

Short Prayer: Jesus, thank You for becoming human. I am so glad I don't have to explain my feelings to a distant God, You already know. Amen.

BLOCK 5: PARENT NOTES (The Secret Weapon)

The Doctrine: The Hypostatic Union (Fully God/Fully Man) This week is about the Incarnation. Jesus is one person with two natures: truly God and truly human. He didn't switch back and forth (sometimes God, sometimes man), and He isn't a mix (a demigod). He is 100% both. This is crucial because if He isn't man, He can't represent us on the cross. If He isn't God, He can't bear the weight of the world's sin.

Why It Matters

- **Sympathy:** We don't pray to a distant force; we pray to a Person who has cried, bled, and felt exhaustion.

- **Salvation:** Only a human can substitute for humans; only God can satisfy God's justice.

- **Example:** Jesus shows us what a perfect human life looks like, dependent on the Father.

Common Misunderstanding to Avoid

- **Misunderstanding:** "Jesus was God wearing a human costume (like a suit)."

  - **Correction**: He was fully human, body, mind, and emotions.

- **Misunderstanding:** "Jesus was half-God, half-man."

  - **Correction**: He was fully both. Infinite and finite, united in one person.

- **Misunderstanding:** "Jesus stopped being God when He came to earth."

  - **Correction**: He humbled Himself, but He never lost His divinity.

How to Answer Follow-Up Questions

- **Q: "Did Jesus know everything when He was a baby?"**

  - A: "As God, He knows everything. But as a human, the Bible says He 'grew in wisdom.' He chose to experience growing up just like us."

- **Q: "Who ran the universe while Jesus was dead?"**

  - A: "God the Father, the Spirit, and the Son (in His divine nature) never stopped being God. His human body died, but God cannot die."

- **Q: "Is He still human now?"**

  - A: "Yes! He rose with a real physical body and is in heaven right now as a man. He will be human forever."

Extra Bible anchors for parents Hebrews 2:17–18; 1 Timothy 2:5; John 1:1; Romans 1:3–4.

Teach-it-back prompt (30-90 seconds) "Hold up two hands. One hand is 'Fully God.' The other is 'Fully Human.' Clasp them together. That's Jesus, one person, two natures. Why do we need Him to be both?"

MEMORY (One-Liner + Catechism Q/A)

One-line definition Jesus is fully God and fully human, so He can understand our weakness and save us from our sin.

Optional Q/A Q: Who is the Redeemer? A: The only Redeemer is the Lord Jesus Christ.

Notes:

WEEK 29: THE CROSS (ATONEMENT)

BLOCK 1: KID PAGE (Big Idea + Anchor Verse)

Big Idea Sin is a big deal that separates us from God, and the penalty for sin is death. Because God is just, He couldn't just ignore our sin, but because He loves us, He didn't want us to die. On the cross, Jesus took the blame for us, dying in our place so we could be forgiven.

Anchor Verse 1 Peter 3:18

In kid words Christ died for sins once and for all, the Good One dying for the bad ones, so He could bring you to God.

Key Words

- **Atonement:** Making two things "at one" again. It means fixing the broken relationship between God and us.

- **Substitute:** Someone who takes the place of another. Jesus was our substitute on the cross.

- **Sacrifice:** Giving up something valuable to pay a cost.

More Bible places to look Isaiah 53:5–6; Romans 5:8; 2 Corinthians 5:21; Mark 10:45; Romans 3:23–26; 1 John 2:2

BLOCK 2: STORY PAGE (Real Life Scenario)

Title: Blame vs. Taking Responsibility   **Setting:** The garage, where tools are scattered everywhere.

The Problem: Caleb was messing around with his dad's expensive drill, even though he wasn't allowed to touch it. He dropped it, and *crack*, the casing split. His stomach dropped. He heard the garage door opening. His instinct was to kick the drill under the workbench and say, "I don't know what happened!" or blame his little brother. The punishment for breaking this would be huge, loss of screens for a month, maybe chores forever.

The Choice Moment: Caleb felt the fear rising. *Hide it,* his brain said. *Run away.* But he knew that was a lie. He looked at the broken drill, then at his dad walking in.

Small Resolution: "Dad," Caleb's voice shook. "I broke the drill. I shouldn't have touched it. I'm sorry." He waited for the yelling. Instead, his dad sighed, picked up the pieces, and looked at Caleb. "Thank you for telling the truth. It's broken, and it costs money to fix. I'm going to pay to fix it, Caleb. I'm taking the cost." Caleb blinked. "But... I broke it." "I know," Dad said. "But I'm your dad. I'll cover it."

Quick Takeaway: Taking responsibility is hard, but Jesus did something even bigger, He took responsibility for things *we* broke.

BLOCK 3: TALK-IT-OUT (Discussion + Coaching)

1. **Understanding:** In the story, who deserved to pay for the drill? Who actually paid for it?

2. **Connection:** Have you ever broken something or made a mistake and tried to hide it? How did that feel?

3. **Application:** The Cross is like Jesus saying, "I will pay for what you broke." How does that make you feel about God?

If your kid says: "Why did Jesus have to die? Couldn't God just say 'I forgive you'?" **Try:** "Imagine a judge who let every criminal go free without punishment. Would he be a good judge? No. God is a good Judge. He has to deal with the wrong things (sin), but He chose to take the punishment Himself."

If your kid says: "That sounds scary/bloody." **Try:** "It is serious. Sin hurts people and offends God. The Cross shows us how serious sin is, but it also shows us how huge God's love is, that He would do that for us."

If your kid says: "I feel bad that Jesus died for me." **Try:** "He didn't do it because you forced Him. He did it because He loves you. He *wanted* to save you. The best way to say thank you is to trust Him."

BLOCK 4: PRACTICE (One Habit This Week)

The Habit: The "My Bad" Practice This week, if you mess up (spill milk, say a mean word, forget a chore), don't make an excuse. Simply say: "I did that. I'm sorry."

When we'll do it: Whenever a mistake happens at home.

What to watch for: Notice how scary it feels to own your mistake, and then remember that Jesus has already paid the ultimate price for your biggest mistakes.

Short Prayer: Jesus, thank You for taking my place. Thank You for paying for my sin so I can be close to God. Help me to be honest when I mess up. Amen.

BLOCK 5: PARENT NOTES (The Secret Weapon)

The Doctrine: Penal Substitutionary Atonement This is the heart of the Gospel. "Penal" means there is a legal penalty for sin (death/judgment). "Substitutionary" means Jesus took that penalty in our place. He lived the perfect life we couldn't live, and died the death we deserved to die. It is the "Great Exchange": He gets our sin; we get His righteousness.

Why It Matters

- **Justice:** It shows God doesn't sweep sin under the rug; He deals with it.

- **Love:** It proves God loves us sacrificially.

- **Security:** If the price is paid, it's paid. We don't have to pay it again.

Common Misunderstanding to Avoid

- **Misunderstanding:** "God is an angry Father taking it out on Jesus."

    - **Correction**: The Father and Son worked together. God didn't punish a third party; He took the penalty Himself through the Son.

- **Misunderstanding:** "Jesus died so I can do whatever I want."

    - **Correction**: He died to free us *from* sin, not *for* sin.

- **Misunderstanding:** "The Cross is just an example of love."

    - **Correction**: It is an example, but first it is a *payment* and a *rescue*.

How to Answer Follow-Up Questions

- **Q: "Did Jesus stay dead?"**

    - A: "No! That's the best part. He paid the bill in full, and then He rose on Sunday. We'll talk about that next week!"

- **Q: "Does the Cross cover sins I haven't done yet?"**

    - A: "Yes. When Jesus died, *all* your sins were in the future. His sacrifice is enough for your whole life."

- **Q: "Why do we use the symbol of a cross?"**

    - A: "To remind us of the price Jesus paid and the victory He won."

Extra Bible anchors for parents Romans 3:25; Galatians 3:13; Hebrews 9:22; 1 Peter 2:24.

Teach-it-back prompt (30-90 seconds) "Put one hand out and say 'My Sin.' Put the other hand out and say 'God's Justice.' Clap them together, that's judgment. Now, put a hand in between them. That's Jesus. He took the clap (the judgment) so we didn't have to."

MEMORY (One-Liner + Catechism Q/A)

One-line definition Jesus died on the cross as our substitute, taking the punishment for our sin so we could be forgiven.

Optional Q/A Q: What kind of death did Christ die? A: The painful and shameful death of the cross.

Notes:

WEEK 30: RESURRECTION

BLOCK 1: KID PAGE (Big Idea + Anchor Verse)

Big Idea Jesus didn't stay dead. On the third day, He rose from the grave with a real body, alive forever. Because He is alive, we know God accepted His payment for sin, and we know that death is not the end of the story for us either.

Anchor Verse 1 Corinthians 15:3–4

In kid words Christ died for our sins, He was buried, and He was raised on the third day, just like the Scriptures said.

Key Words

- **Resurrection:** Coming back to life in a body that will never die again.

- **Victory:** Winning a battle. Jesus won the battle against sin and death.

- **Hope:** Knowing for sure that good things are coming because of what God has done.

More Bible places to look Matthew 28:5–6; Luke 24:36–43; John 11:25–26; Romans 6:9; 1 Peter 1:3; Revelation 1:18

BLOCK 2: STORY PAGE (Real Life Scenario)

Title: Discouraged After the Loss

Setting: The locker room after the biggest baseball game of the season.

The Problem: The score was 5–4. They lost. Jordan sat on the bench, staring at his cleats. They had practiced so hard. He had prayed they would win. Now it was over. It felt like the whole season was a waste. "What's the point?" he muttered. "We lost. It's done." It felt like a heavy curtain had dropped, ending everything good.

The Choice Moment: Jordan could stay grumpy and believe that losing this game meant everything was ruined. Or he could listen to his coach, who was standing by the door.

Small Resolution: "Heads up, guys," Coach said. "This hurts. But this isn't the end of your baseball career. It's one game. We come back next season. The story isn't over." Jordan looked up. It still hurt, but he realized Coach was right. The loss felt final, but it wasn't *final* final.

Quick Takeaway: Losing feels terrible, but the Resurrection tells us that even the worst thing (death) isn't the end of the story.

BLOCK 3: TALK-IT-OUT (Discussion + Coaching)

1. **Understanding:** Coach said there is a "next season," but Jesus says there is a "forever life." How is Jesus' victory better than just winning a game?

2. **Connection:** Have you ever had a really sad day where it felt like nothing would ever be good again?

3. **Application:** How does knowing Jesus is alive help us when we are sad or scared about death?

If your kid says: "Is Jesus a ghost/zombie?" **Try:** "No, zombies are pretend monsters that are dead but moving. Jesus is fully alive with a healthy, perfect body. He ate fish and let his friends touch his hands. He is more alive than we are!"

If your kid says: "Why did He wait three days?" **Try:** "To prove He was really dead. If He came back in five minutes, people might say He just fainted. Three days proved the miracle was real."

If your kid says: "Will we have bodies in heaven?" **Try:** "Someday, yes! When Jesus comes back, we will be resurrected just like Him, with real bodies that can run and hug and eat, but will never get sick or die."

BLOCK 4: PRACTICE (One Habit This Week)

The Habit: The Sunday Celebration Every Sunday is a "mini-Easter." This Sunday, wake up and say, "Happy Sunday! Jesus is alive!"

When we'll do it: First thing Sunday morning.

What to watch for: See if starting the day with that truth changes how you feel about going to church or worshiping.

Short Prayer: God, thank You that the tomb is empty. Thank You that Jesus is alive right now. Because He lives, I can have hope even on bad days. Amen.

BLOCK 5: PARENT NOTES (The Secret Weapon)

The Doctrine: The Resurrection The Resurrection is the pivot point of history. If Jesus stayed dead, our faith is useless (1 Cor. 15:17). The fact that He rose means: 1) He is who He said He was (God), 2) The penalty for sin was accepted (the check cleared), and 3) He has defeated death. It's not just a spiritual idea; it was a physical event in history.

Why It Matters

- **Validation:** It proves Jesus wasn't just a nice teacher; He conquered the grave.

- **Future Hope:** We will follow in His footsteps. Our bodies matter to God.

- **Power:** The same power that raised Jesus lives in believers (Eph. 1:19-20).

Common Misunderstanding to Avoid

- **Misunderstanding:** "Jesus rose in people's hearts/memories."

    ○ **Correction**: The tomb was empty. His physical body was gone and walking around. It was real.

- **Misunderstanding:** "We turn into angels when we die."

    ○ **Correction**: Angels are different creatures. We are humans, and we will be resurrected humans.

- **Misunderstanding:** "Science proves miracles can't happen."

    ○ **Correction**: Science studies the natural world. God is the Author of the story; He can change the plot whenever He wants.

How to Answer Follow-Up Questions

- **Q: "Where is Jesus' body now?"**

    ○ A: "He is in Heaven with God the Father. A real man is sitting on the throne of the universe right now."

- **Q: "Did it hurt to come back to life?"**

    ○ A: "The Bible doesn't say, but it seems like it was glorious and powerful, not painful."

- **Q: "What if I'm scared of dying?"**

    ○ A: "That is normal. But Jesus has gone through death first. He punched a hole in the scary wall of death so He could hold your hand and walk you through to the other side."

Extra Bible anchors for parents Acts 2:24; Romans 4:25; 1 Corinthians 15:20–22; Philippians 3:21.

Teach-it-back prompt (30-90 seconds) "Play 'Dead or Alive.' I'll say a name (Abraham Lincoln, Moses, Grandma's dog). You say 'Dead' (their body is still in the ground). When I say 'Jesus,' you shout 'ALIVE!' Why is He different?"

MEMORY (One-Liner + Catechism Q/A)

One-line definition On the third day, Jesus physically rose from the dead, defeating sin and death forever.

Optional Q/A Q: Did Christ remain in the grave? A: No, He rose bodily from the grave on the third day.

Notes:

WEEK 31: SALVATION: REPENTANCE & FAITH

BLOCK 1: KID PAGE (Big Idea + Anchor Verse)

Big Idea How do we get the gift Jesus bought for us? We don't earn it. We turn away from our sin (Repentance) and turn toward Jesus, trusting Him to save us (Faith). These two things, turning from sin and trusting Jesus, are like two sides of the same coin.

Anchor Verse Mark 1:15

In kid words The time has come! The kingdom of God is near. Turn away from your sins and believe the good news!

Key Words

- **Repentance:** A change of mind and heart. It means turning around, walking away from sin and toward God.

- **Faith:** Trusting Jesus. It's not just knowing *about* Him, but relying *on* Him.

- **Conversion:** The moment when someone turns to Jesus and becomes a Christian.

More Bible places to look Acts 3:19; Romans 10:9; Ephesians 2:8–9; 1 John 1:9; Acts 16:31; Joel 2:13

BLOCK 2: STORY PAGE (Real Life Scenario)

Title: Saying Sorry First

Setting: The driveway basketball hoop.

The Problem: Ty and his friend Mason were yelling. "You fouled me!" "I didn't! You just missed!" Ty shoved Mason. Mason shoved back. Ty threw the ball into the bushes and stomped inside. He was so mad. He sat on his bed, replaying the moment. *Mason started it,* he thought. *He should apologize to me.* But deep down, Ty knew he shouldn't have shoved. He shouldn't have thrown the ball.

The Choice Moment: Ty could stay in his room and wait for Mason to apologize (which might take forever), or he could swallow his pride, go back outside, and own his part of the mess.

Small Resolution: Ty took a breath. He walked outside. Mason was sitting on the curb. "I shouldn't have shoved you," Ty said. "That was wrong. I'm sorry." Mason looked up, surprised. "Yeah. I shouldn't have shoved back. Sorry." They were okay again. Ty had to turn away from his anger to fix the friendship.

Quick Takeaway: To fix a relationship, you have to admit you were wrong and turn back to the person. That is what repentance looks like with God.

BLOCK 3: TALK-IT-OUT (Discussion + Coaching)

1. **Understanding:** Why is it hard to say "I was wrong" first?

2. **Connection:** Is there something you know is wrong (a sin) that you are holding onto instead of turning away from?

3. **Application:** Faith is like leaning your whole weight on a chair. How do we "lean" on Jesus instead of our own goodness?

If your kid says: "I say sorry to God, but I keep doing the same bad thing. Am I not saved?" **Try:** "Repentance is a lifelong habit, not a one-time thing. It's like washing your hands, you do it every time you get dirty. God sees your heart. Keep turning back to Him."

If your kid says: "I believe in Jesus, but I don't *feel* different." **Try:** "Faith isn't a feeling; it's a choice to trust. If you are trusting Jesus to save you, you are saved, even on days you feel grumpy or plain."

If your kid says: "Is faith just believing God is real?" **Try:** "It's more than that. The devil knows God is real! Faith is trusting God is *for you* and relying on Him. Like trusting a parachute, not just believing parachutes exist."

BLOCK 4: PRACTICE (One Habit This Week)

The Habit: The U-Turn Prayer Picture a "U-Turn" sign. When you realize you are heading the wrong way (sin, anger, selfishness), pray: "God, I am making a U-Turn back to You."

When we'll do it: When we get caught in a bad attitude or a lie.

What to watch for: Notice that God isn't standing there with a stick waiting to hit you; He is like the father in the Prodigal Son story, waiting with open arms.

Short Prayer: God, I want to turn away from my sin and trust You. Thank You that whenever I turn back to You, You are ready to welcome me. Amen.

BLOCK 5: PARENT NOTES (The Secret Weapon)

The Doctrine: Conversion (Repentance & Faith) Salvation requires a response. We are not saved *by* our repentance (Jesus saves us), but repentance and faith are the empty hands that receive the gift.

- **Repentance** is the negative side: Turning *from* sin.

- **Faith** is the positive side: Turning *to* Christ. You cannot truly have one without the other.

Why It Matters

- **Ownership:** It moves faith from "my parents' religion" to "my trust in Jesus."

- **Humility:** It admits we are wrong and need help.

- **Relationship:** It restores the closeness that sin broke.

Common Misunderstanding to Avoid

- **Misunderstanding:** "Repentance means cleaning up my life *before* I come to Jesus."

  - **Correction**: No, we come to Him messy, and He cleans us up.

- **Misunderstanding:** "Faith is blind optimism."

  - **Correction**: Faith is trust based on evidence, the life and resurrection of Jesus.

- **Misunderstanding:** "I repented once when I was 5, so I'm done."

  - **Correction**: We are justified once, but we live a life of repentance.

How to Answer Follow-Up Questions

- **Q: "How much faith do I need?"**

  - A: "Jesus said even faith as small as a mustard seed is enough. It's not about the size of your faith; it's about the strength of the Person you trust."

- **Q: "What if I doubt?"**

  - A: "Doubts are normal. Bring them to God. You can say, 'I believe, help my unbelief!'"

- **Q: "Why do I have to say sorry if God already knows?"**

  - A: "Because admitting it changes *your* heart. It keeps you honest and humble."

Extra Bible anchors for parents Psalm 51:1–4; Isaiah 55:7; Luke 15:11–24 (Prodigal Son); Ephesians 2:8.

Teach-it-back prompt (30-90 seconds) "Stand in the middle of the room. Walk toward a wall (label it 'Sin'). Stop. Turn around 180 degrees. Walk toward the other wall (label it 'Jesus'). That turn is repentance. Walking to Jesus is faith."

MEMORY (One-Liner + Catechism Q/A)

One-line definition Salvation comes when we turn away from our sin (repentance) and trust in Jesus alone to save us (faith).

Optional Q/A Q: What is faith in Jesus Christ? A: Receiving and resting on Him alone for salvation.

Notes:

WEEK 32: JUSTIFICATION & ADOPTION

BLOCK 1: KID PAGE (Big Idea + Anchor Verse)

Big Idea When we trust Jesus, God does two amazing things instantly. First, He declares us "Not Guilty" (Justification). Second, He adopts us into His family (Adoption). You aren't just a forgiven criminal; you are a beloved child of the King.

Anchor Verse Romans 8:15

In kid words You didn't receive a spirit that makes you a slave to fear. Instead, you received the Spirit of adoption, by whom we cry out, "Abba, Father!"

Key Words

- **Justification:** A judge's legal decision. God looks at us and says, "Righteous!" because of Jesus.

- **Adoption:** A father's legal decision. God brings us into His family and gives us His name.

- **Righteousness:** Being right with God. Jesus gives us His perfect record.

More Bible places to look Romans 3:23–24; Galatians 4:4–7; 1 John 3:1; Romans 5:1; 2 Corinthians 5:21; Ephesians 1:5

BLOCK 2: STORY PAGE (Real Life Scenario)

Title: Feeling "Not Enough"   **Setting:** Before school, looking in the mirror.

The Problem: Chloe was brushing her hair, staring at herself. *I'm not as pretty as Sarah,* she thought. *And I'm not smart like Ben.* She remembered yelling at her brother yesterday. *And I'm not even a very good person.* A heavy feeling settled in her chest. She felt like she had to work super hard just to be "okay," but she was failing. She felt like an outsider in her own life.

The Choice Moment: She could listen to the voice that said, "You aren't enough; try harder." Or she could remember what her mom told her about who she was.

Small Resolution: Chloe put down the brush. She whispered, "I am a child of God." It felt weird to say it to the mirror. "God loves me right now." She didn't suddenly feel like a supermodel or a genius, but the heavy weight lifted a little bit. She didn't have to earn her place. She was already in the family.

Quick Takeaway: You don't have to earn your way into God's family; Jesus opens the door, and the Father welcomes you in.

BLOCK 3: TALK-IT-OUT (Discussion + Coaching)

1. **Understanding:** What is the difference between a judge saying "You are free to go" and a father saying "Welcome home"?

2. **Connection:** Do you ever feel like you have to be "good enough" for God to love you? When?

3. **Application:** "Abba" is an Aramaic word like "Dad" or "Papa." How does it feel to know you can call the Creator of the Universe "Papa"?

If your kid says: "But I still sin. How can God say I'm righteous?" **Try:** "Imagine you took a test and got an F, but Jesus took the test and got an A+. Justification means Jesus puts His name on your test. God looks at Jesus' score, not yours."

If your kid says: "Is being adopted weird?" **Try:** "Adoption is beautiful! It means you were chosen on purpose. In Roman times, an adopted son had all the same rights as a born son. Nothing was held back."

If your kid says: "I don't feel special." **Try:** "Feelings go up and down like a roller coaster. God's promise is like the track, it stays solid. You are His child whether you feel like it or not."

BLOCK 4: PRACTICE (One Habit This Week)

The Habit: The Name Tag Imagine you are wearing a name tag that says "Child of God."

When we'll do it: When you feel left out, embarrassed, or like a failure.

What to watch for: Remind yourself: "It doesn't matter what others think. The King is my Father. I belong to Him."

Short Prayer: Father God, thank You for adopting me. Thank You that I don't have to perform to earn Your love. I am safe because I am Yours. Amen.

BLOCK 5: PARENT NOTES (The Secret Weapon)

The Doctrine: Justification & Adoption This is the "Double Cure."

- **Justification** deals with our guilt. We are declared righteous in God's court.

- **Adoption** deals with our estrangement. We are brought into God's living room. We are not just acquitted criminals; we are heirs.

Why it matters

- **Security:** If you are adopted, you can't be "un-childed" because of a bad day.

- **Prayer:** We come to God not as a boss, but as a Father.

- **Identity:** Our worth isn't in our grades, sports, or looks, but in our status as God's children.

Common misunderstandings to avoid

- **Misunderstanding:** "Justification makes me perfect instantly." (Correction: It changes your *status*, not your *behavior*. Behavior change "Sanctification" takes a lifetime.)

- **Misunderstanding:** "God only loves me when I'm good." (Correction: He loves you because you are His child, period.)

- **Misunderstanding:** "We are all God's children." (Correction: All humans are God's *creation*, but only those who trust Jesus are adopted as His *children*.)

How to answer follow-up questions

- **Q: "Can I get kicked out of the family?"**

  - A: "No. Jesus said, 'No one can snatch them out of my hand.' You are secure."

- **Q: "Why does God discipline us if we are forgiven?"**

  - A: "Because He is a good Dad. He disciplines us to train us and keep us safe, not to pay us back for our sins. Jesus already paid."

- **Q: "Is Jesus my brother?"**

  - A: "Technically, yes! The Bible calls Him the 'firstborn among many brothers.' He is our King, but also our big Brother."

Extra Bible anchors for parents Romans 8:1; Romans 8:14–17; Galatians 3:26; 1 John 3:1–2.

Teach-it-back prompt (30-90 seconds) "Get a jacket. Put it on your kid. Say: 'This is Jesus' righteousness.' Now look at them and say, 'When God looks at you, He sees Jesus' goodness covering you. You are accepted!'"

<u>MEMORY (One-Liner + Catechism Q/A)</u>

One-line definition God declares us not guilty (Justification) and adopts us as His own children (Adoption) because of what Jesus did.

Optional Q/A Q: What is adoption? A: God receiving us into His family and giving us all the privileges of His children.

<u>Notes:</u>

WEEK 33: REVIEW: THE GOSPEL IN ONE PAGE

BLOCK 1: KID PAGE (Big Idea + Anchor Verse)

Big Idea The Gospel simply means "Good News." It is the story of how God saves us through Jesus. We've learned a lot of big words lately (Incarnation, Atonement, Resurrection), but they all fit together into one amazing message: God saves sinners.

Anchor Verse Ephesians 2:8–9

In kid words You are saved by grace through faith. It is not something you did to earn it; it is a gift from God so no one can brag.

Key Words

- **Gospel:** Good News.

- **Grace:** Getting a good gift you do not deserve.

- **Mercy:** NOT getting the punishment you DO deserve.

More Bible places to look Romans 1:16; 1 Corinthians 15:1–4; Titus 3:4–5; John 3:16; Romans 6:23

BLOCK 2: STORY PAGE (Real Life Scenario)

Title: The Group Project Slacker

Setting: A classroom with desks pushed together.

The Problem: Liam was furious. He had done the entire poster. He did the research. He drew the map. His partner, Noah, had done *nothing* except draw doodles in the corner. The teacher walked by. "Great job, boys," she said. She gave the poster an 'A'. Noah grinned. "Sweet! We got an A!" Liam wanted to scream. "You didn't do anything!" he thought. "I did the work! You got my grade!"

The Choice Moment: Liam felt the unfairness burning in his chest. But then a thought hit him. In this project, *he* was the worker and Noah was the slacker. But in real life with God, *Jesus* did the work, and Liam was the one getting the free A.

Small Resolution: Liam took a deep breath. It wasn't fair. Noah didn't deserve the A. "Yeah," Liam said quietly. "We got an A." He didn't rub it in. He realized that with God, *he* was the slacker who got Jesus' grade.

Quick Takeaway: Grace means getting the "A" that Jesus earned, even though we didn't do the work.

BLOCK 3: TALK-IT-OUT (Discussion + Coaching)

1. **Understanding:** Why was Liam mad at first? How is the "A" on the poster like salvation?

2. **Connection:** Is it hard for you to accept gifts you didn't earn? Why or why not?

3. **Application:** If the Gospel is true, how should we treat other people when they mess up?

If your kid says: "That's not fair! Noah should have done work." **Try:** "You are right. It isn't fair. Grace isn't fair. If God were fair, we would all be in big trouble. Mercy is better than fairness."

If your kid says: "Can I explain the Gospel in my own words?" **Try:** "Yes! Try this pattern: God (is holy), Man (sinned), Christ (paid the price), Response (faith). Try using those four words."

If your kid says: "I forget the Gospel sometimes." **Try:** "We all do. That's why we go to church, read the Bible, and take Communion. To remember the Good News over and over."

BLOCK 4: PRACTICE (One Habit This Week)

The Habit: The Gospel Replay Every night this week, before you sleep, finish this sentence: "I am loved not because I was good today, but because..."

When we'll do it: Bedtime.

What to watch for: The answer should always be about Jesus (He died for me, He is good), not about you (I did my chores, I was nice).

Short Prayer: Lord, thank You for the Gospel. Thank You that I don't have to save myself. Thank You for doing all the work so I could be with You. Amen.

BLOCK 5: PARENT NOTES (The Secret Weapon)

The Doctrine: The Gospel (Summary) This week is a "catch-up" to solidify Weeks 28–32. The Gospel is news, not advice. Advice says, "Here is what you should do." News says, "Here is what has been done for you." Structure to remember:

1. **Creation:** God made us for relationship.

2. **Fall:** We sinned and broke it.

3. **Redemption:** Jesus lived, died, and rose to fix it.

4. **Restoration:** We trust Him and are restored.

Why It Matters

- **Confidence:** It moves the focus off our performance and onto Jesus' finished work.

- **Motivation:** We obey God out of gratitude, not fear.

- **Sharing:** You can't share the faith if you can't summarize it.

Common Misunderstanding to Avoid

- **Misunderstanding:** "The Gospel is the ABCs of Christianity; now I need the deep stuff."

  - **Correction**: The Gospel is the A-to-Z. We never graduate from it.

- **Misunderstanding:** "The Gospel is just 'be nice like Jesus'."

  - **Correction**: That's the *result* of the Gospel. The Gospel is that Jesus died for people who *aren't* nice.

- **Misunderstanding:** "I have to be good to keep my salvation."

  - **Correction**: You are kept by grace, just like you were saved by grace.

How to Answer Follow-Up Questions

- **Q: "Why is it called Good News?"**

  - A: "Because 'bad news' is that we are stuck in sin. The 'good news' is that the rescue has arrived!"

- **Q: "Do I have to know all the big words to be saved?"**

  - A: "Nope. The thief on the cross didn't know the word 'justification.' He just knew Jesus could save him."

Extra Bible anchors for parents 1 Corinthians 15:3–4; Romans 5:8; Ephesians 2:1–10.

Teach-it-back prompt (30-90 seconds) "Draw a cliff on a piece of paper. Draw a stick figure on one side (Us) and God on the other. Draw a cross bridging the gap. Ask: 'Can the stick figure jump across? No. Who made the bridge? Jesus. That is the Gospel.'"

MEMORY (One-Liner + Catechism Q/A)

One-line definition The Gospel is the good news that Jesus lived, died, and rose again to save sinners like us.

Optional Q/A Q: What is the Gospel? A: The good news of salvation through Jesus Christ.

Notes:

WEEK 34: LIFE SKILL: COURAGE

BLOCK 1: KID PAGE (Big Idea + Anchor Verse)

Big Idea Because Jesus is with us, we don't have to be afraid of what people think or what might happen. Christian courage isn't about not feeling fear; it is about obeying God even when your knees are shaking.

Anchor Verse Joshua 1:9

In kid words Be strong and courageous. Do not be afraid or discouraged, because the Lord your God is with you wherever you go.

Key Words

- **Courage:** Doing the right thing even when you are scared.

- **Fear of Man:** Being more worried about what people think than what God thinks.

- **Boldness:** Confidence to speak the truth.

More Bible places to look Psalm 27:1; Psalm 56:3; Proverbs 29:25; Acts 4:13; 2 Timothy 1:7; Hebrews 13:6

BLOCK 2: STORY PAGE (Real Life Scenario)

Title: The Inside Joke

Setting: The back of the school bus.

The Problem: A group of popular kids was laughing. They were making fun of a girl named Tara, whispering an "inside joke" about her shoes. One of the popular boys looked at Ethan. "Hey Ethan, look at those boots. Space ranger, right?" He laughed. Ethan wanted to laugh. He wanted to be part of the group. He felt the pull to just smile and nod so he wouldn't be the weird o ne out.

The Choice Moment: Ethan's heart beat fast. If he didn't laugh, they might make fun of *him*. But he knew it was mean. He knew Jesus wouldn't laugh.

Small Resolution: Ethan didn't laugh. He looked at the boy and shrugged. "I think they're fine," he said quietly. Then he turned around in his seat. It got quiet for a second. The boy rolled his eyes. "Whatever." Ethan felt shaky, but he also felt clean. He hadn't joined in.

Quick Takeaway: Courage sometimes looks like staying quiet when everyone else is laughing, or speaking up when everyone else is quiet.

<u>BLOCK 3: TALK-IT-OUT (Discussion + Coaching)</u>

1. **Understanding:** Why was it scary for Ethan to not laugh? What did he risk?

2. **Connection:** Have you ever felt pressured to do something wrong just to fit in?

3. **Application:** How does knowing "Jesus is with you" help you be brave on the school bus or at practice?

If your kid says: "I'm just a kid. I can't stand up to bullies." **Try:** "You don't have to be a superhero. Sometimes courage is just walking away, or telling a teacher. Or sitting next to the person being teased."

If your kid says: "What if I lose my friends?" **Try:** "That is a real scary thought. But a friend who requires you to be mean isn't a good friend. God will help you find true friends."

If your kid says: "I feel scared all the time." **Try:** "That's okay. Courage counts most when you are scared. Talk to Jesus about your fear. He is the Lion of Judah; He can share His bravery with you."

<u>BLOCK 4: PRACTICE (One Habit This Week)</u>

The Habit: The "God is Bigger" Breath When you feel scared (of the dark, a test, or a person), take a deep breath. Breathe out the fear. Breathe in the truth: "God is bigger than this."

When we'll do it: Before a hard conversation or a scary moment.

What to watch for: Notice how your body relaxes when you remember God is right there with you.

Short Prayer: Jesus, You were brave when people hated You. Help me to be brave too. I want to care more about what You think than what other people think. Amen.

<u>BLOCK 5: PARENT NOTES (The Secret Weapon)</u>

The Doctrine: The Fear of the Lord vs. Fear of Man Courage comes from re-ordering our fears. If we fear (respect/awe) God most, we won't fear people as much. If we fear people most, we will constantly disobey God to please them. Jesus is the ultimate example of courage, He set His face like flint toward the cross (Isaiah 50:7).

Why It Matters

- **Integrity:** You can't be honest if you are terrified of people's reactions.

- **Witness:** A courageous kid stands out. People notice when someone doesn't follow the crowd.

- **Peace:** Fearing man is a trap (Prov. 29:25); trusting God brings safety.

Common Misunderstanding to Avoid

- **Misunderstanding:** "Courage means I'm never scared."

  - **Correction**: Courage *requires* fear. If you aren't scared, you don't need courage. It means acting *despite* the fear.

- **Misunderstanding:** "Being brave means being loud or fighting."

  - **Correction**: Sometimes bravery is quiet gentleness in the face of anger.

- **Misunderstanding:** "If I'm brave, nothing bad will happen."

  - **Correction**: You might still get teased. But you will have peace with God, which is better.

How to Answer Follow-Up Questions

- **Q: "Was Jesus ever scared?"**

  - A: "In the Garden of Gethsemane, He was very distressed about the cross. But He obeyed anyway. That is perfect courage."

- **Q: "How do I get more brave?"**

  - A: "By knowing God better. The bigger God gets in your eyes, the smaller the scary things look."

Extra Bible anchors for parents Psalm 118:6; Matthew 10:28; Acts 4:29; Hebrews 13:5–6.

Teach-it-back prompt (30-90 seconds) "Hold a pebble close to your eye. It blocks your whole view, right? That's a problem (like a bully). Now hold the pebble at arm's length and look at the whole room (God). The pebble is still there, but it's small compared to the room. Keep your eyes on the Big Room (God)."

<u>MEMORY (One-Liner + Catechism Q/A)</u>

One-line definition Courage is doing what is right even when we are afraid, because we know God is with us.

Optional Q/A Q: What does God tell us about fear? A: Do not fear, for I am with you.

<u>Notes:</u>

WEEK 35: LIFE SKILL: LOVE YOUR NEIGHBOR

BLOCK 1: KID PAGE (Big Idea + Anchor Verse)

Big Idea Jesus taught that the second greatest commandment is to "love your neighbor as yourself." Love isn't just a warm feeling; it is an action. It means treating others with the same care, kindness, and help that you would want for yourself.

Anchor Verse Mark 12:30–31

In kid words Love the Lord your God with all your heart... and love your neighbor as yourself. There is no command greater than these.

Key Words

- **Neighbor:** Anyone you are around. Not just the person next door, but the kid at school, the person at the store, and even someone you don't like.

- **Selfless:** Thinking of others before yourself.

- **Compassion:** Seeing someone's need and wanting to help.

More Bible places to look Luke 10:25–37 (Good Samaritan); John 13:34–35; Romans 13:10; 1 John 4:11; Galatians 5:14

BLOCK 2: STORY PAGE (Real Life Scenario)

Title: Serving Someone Left Out   **Setting:** Recess, near the four-square courts.

The Problem: Everyone was rushing to get in line for four-square. Mia saw a new girl, Ava, standing by the fence, looking at her shoes. Ava didn't speak much English yet and didn't have any friends. Mia wanted to play. If she got out of line to talk to Ava, she would lose her spot. She would miss the game.

The Choice Moment: *I can pretend I didn't see her,* Mia thought. *It's not my fault she's alone.* But the Holy Spirit nudged her heart. "Love your neighbor."

Small Resolution: Mia sighed, stepped out of line, and walked over to the fence. "Hi," Mia said. "I'm Mia. Do you want to watch the game with me? I can show you how to play." Ava looked up and smiled a tiny, shy smile. "Okay." Mia missed the game, but she made a friend.

Quick Takeaway: Loving your neighbor usually costs something (time, a turn, a game), but it shows Jesus' love to them.

BLOCK 3: TALK-IT-OUT (Discussion + Coaching)

1. **Understanding:** What did it cost Mia to love her neighbor? Was it worth it?

2. **Connection:** Who is a "neighbor" in your life right now who might need kindness? (Think of school, sports, or family).

3. **Application:** How can you love your neighbor this week with your actions, not just your words?

If your kid says: "Do I have to like them to love them?" **Try:** "No. 'Like' is a feeling that comes and goes. 'Love' is a choice to seek their good. You can treat someone valuable and help them even if they annoy you. That is actually the strongest kind of love."

If your kid says: "What if they are mean to me?" **Try:** "Jesus said to love our enemies. It stops the cycle of mean-ness. You can be kind without letting them bully you."

If your kid says: "I don't have any money to help people." **Try:** "Love isn't usually about money. It's about attention. Listening, inviting, smiling, and helping carry things are all free."

BLOCK 4: PRACTICE (One Habit This Week)

The Habit: The "You First" Rule Pick one time each day to let someone else go first. First to get a snack, first out the door, first to choose a TV show.

When we'll do it: Once a day, intentionally.

What to watch for: Notice if it feels hard to give up your spot. That feeling is selfishness dying and love growing!

Short Prayer: Jesus, You loved us when we were unlovely. Help me to see the people around me and love them like You do. Help me put others first. Amen.

BLOCK 5: PARENT NOTES (The Secret Weapon)

The Doctrine: The Royal Law (Love) The Bible calls "Love your neighbor as yourself" the Royal Law (James 2:8). It is the evidence of true faith. We cannot claim to love God (whom we haven't seen) if we hate our brother (whom we have seen) (1 John 4:20).

Why It Matters

- **Witness:** Jesus said people will know we are His disciples by our love.

- **Unity:** Love binds the church together.

- **Happiness:** Ironically, focusing on self brings misery; focusing on others brings joy.

Common Misunderstanding to Avoid

- **Misunderstanding:** "Love means agreeing with everything someone does."

  ○ **Correction**: You can love someone deeply while disagreeing with their choices. God does this with us.

- **Misunderstanding:** "Love is just being nice."

  ○ **Correction**: Love is active. It seeks the good of the other. Sometimes love is tough; sometimes it is sacrificial.

- **Misunderstanding:** "I have to ignore my own needs."

  ○ **Correction**: The command is "as yourself." You care for yourself (eat, sleep), and you should extend that same care to others.

How to Answer Follow-Up Questions

- **Q: "Who is my neighbor?"**

  ○ A: "Jesus told the Good Samaritan story to answer that. Your neighbor is anyone God puts in your path who has a need."

- **Q: "Why is it so hard?"**

  ○ A: "Because we are born selfish. Sin curves us inward. The Holy Spirit helps us curve outward toward others."

Extra Bible anchors for parents Leviticus 19:18; Luke 6:27–31; Romans 12:9–10; 1 Corinthians 13.

Teach-it-back prompt (30-90 seconds) "Think of a mirror. When you look in it, you see yourself. Love is like turning the mirror into a window so you can see the person standing next to you. Who can you 'see' today?"

MEMORY (One-Liner + Catechism Q/A)

One-line definition We love our neighbors by treating them with the same kindness and care that we want for ourselves.

Optional Q/A Q: What is the second commandment? A: You shall love your neighbor as yourself.

Notes:

WEEK 36: SEASONAL/FLEX: EASTER / RESURRECTION CELEBRATION

BLOCK 1: KID PAGE (Big Idea + Anchor Verse)

Big Idea Easter is the biggest celebration of the year for Christians. It is the day we remember that Jesus punched a hole through death and came out the other side alive! Because He lives, we have joy that no one can take away.

Anchor Verse Revelation 1:17–18

In kid words Do not be afraid. I am the First and the Last, and the Living One. I was dead, but look, I am alive forever and ever, and I hold the keys of death.

Key Words

- **Hallelujah:** A Hebrew word that means "Praise the Lord!"

- **Triumph:** A great victory or success.

- **Firstfruits:** Jesus is the first one to be resurrected; we will follow Him later.

More Bible places to look Matthew 28:1–10; Luke 24:1–12; John 20:1–18; 1 Corinthians 15:54–57

BLOCK 2: STORY PAGE (Real Life Scenario)

Title: The Easter Morning Question

Setting: Driving to church on Easter morning, everyone dressed in nice clothes.

The Problem: "Why do we have to dress up?" Ben asked, tugging at his tie. "And why is church so long on Easter?" It just felt like a lot of extra work. Candy was fun, but the rest of it felt boring. He didn't get why the grownups were so excited. "It happened a long time ago," Ben said. "Why is it such a big deal today?"

The Choice Moment: His big sister, Sarah, looked back. She could have been annoyed, but she remembered how scary it was when Grandma died last year. "Ben," she said. "Remember Grandma?"

Small Resolution: Ben got quiet. "Yeah." "Because of Easter," Sarah said, "we will see her again. Jesus beat death. If He didn't rise, then... death wins. But He did. So we celebrate because death is broken." Ben stopped tugging his tie. He looked out the window. "Oh," he said. "That is a big deal."

Quick Takeaway: We celebrate Easter with joy because it means death is not the boss of us, Jesus is.

BLOCK 3: TALK-IT-OUT (Discussion + Coaching)

1. **Understanding:** Why did connecting Easter to Grandma help Ben understand?

2. **Connection:** What is your favorite part of Easter? The candy? The songs? The story?

3. **Application:** If Jesus is alive right now, what does that mean for us today? (He can hear us, He can help us, He is with us).

If your kid says: "Is the Easter Bunny real?" **Try:** "The Easter Bunny is a fun game, like Santa, but he isn't real. The real excitement is Jesus. Bunnies and eggs remind us of new life (spring), but Jesus is the true New Life."

If your kid says: "Why do we say 'He is Risen'?" **Try:** "It's an old church password! One person says 'He is Risen!' and the other answers 'He is Risen Indeed!' It reminds us we are on the same team."

If your kid says: "I don't feel happy today." **Try:** "That's okay. The first Easter started with people crying and scared at a tomb. Joy came later. Jesus loves you even if you are grumpy."

BLOCK 4: PRACTICE (One Habit This Week)

The Habit: The Easter Greeting Teach your family the "Password." Person A: "He is Risen!" Person B: "He is Risen Indeed!"

When we'll do it: All day on Easter Sunday (or any Sunday!).

What to watch for: Feel the connection with millions of Christians all over the world saying the same words in different languages.

Short Prayer: Jesus, You are the Living One! You have the keys to death and the grave. I praise You because You are alive and You are my King. Hallelujah! Amen.

BLOCK 5: PARENT NOTES (The Secret Weapon)

The Doctrine: Christian Hope (Celebration) Easter isn't just a historical commemoration; it is a feast of Hope. The Resurrection vindicated Jesus, justified sinners, and guaranteed our future resurrection. We celebrate not just that He lives, but that *because* He lives, we shall live also (John 14:19).

Why It Matters

- **Perspective:** It shrinks our current problems. If death is defeated, what can really hurt us?

- **Joy:** Christianity is the only religion with a singing, feasting joy at its center because our Hero won.

- **Mission:** We have good news to tell a dying world.

Common Misunderstanding to Avoid

- **Misunderstanding:** "Easter is about spring and flowers."

  ○ **Correction**: Those are symbols of new life, but the *cause* is the empty tomb.

- **Misunderstanding:** "It's just a story to make us feel better about dying."

  ○ **Correction**: Paul says if it's just a story, we are to be pitied (1 Cor. 15:19). We believe it is a fact.

How to Answer Follow-Up Questions

- **Q: "Why did they kill Him?"**

    - A: "The religious leaders were jealous, and the Romans were afraid of a riot. But really, it was God's plan to save us."

- **Q: "Can I be baptized on Easter?"**

    - A: "Many people are! Baptism shows exactly what Easter is, going down into death and coming up to new life."

Extra Bible anchors for parents Job 19:25; Psalm 16:10; Acts 2:22–32; Colossians 3:1–4.

Teach-it-back prompt (30-90 seconds) "Make a fist (Stone). Cover it with your other hand (Tomb). Say 'Friday... Saturday...'. Then pop the fist open: 'SUNDAY!' The stone is rolled away. The tomb is open. He is out!"

MEMORY (One-Liner + Catechism Q/A)

One-line definition We celebrate Easter because Jesus defeated death and is alive forevermore!

Optional Q/A Q: Why is the resurrection important? A: It proves Jesus is God and guarantees our own resurrection.

Notes:

Part 5: Holy Spirit & Growth

At this point, a really honest question shows up in most homes: "Okay... but how do we actually change?"

That's what this part is for.

We'll talk about the **Holy Spirit**, prayer, spiritual habits, and fighting temptation... because willpower runs out, and kids need to know they have a **Helper** who empowers them from the inside out.

Each week is meant to feel practical, not preachy. You'll give your kids language for the battle, tools for the moment they feel pulled toward sin, and a pathway for growth that doesn't rely on pretending they're fine.

The win here is steady: not instant perfection, but real progress... learning to live like Jesus with help that's actually strong enough.

WEEK 37: THE HOLY SPIRIT

BLOCK 1: KID PAGE (Big Idea + Anchor Verse)

Big Idea God the Father and God the Son are in heaven, but God the Holy Spirit is right here with us. He is not a ghost or a force like electricity; He is a real Person who helps us, comforts us, and points us to Jesus. We are never alone because He lives inside everyone who trusts in Jesus.

Anchor Verse *John 14:26* **In kid words:** Jesus promised that the Father would send the Holy Spirit to teach us and remind us of everything Jesus said.

Key Words

- **Helper:** Another name for the Holy Spirit (Jesus called Him the "Paraclete," which means someone called to walk beside you).

- **Indwelling:** A big word meaning the Holy Spirit lives inside believers like a home.

More Bible places to look: Acts 2:1–4; Romans 8:26; 1 Corinthians 3:16; Galatians 5:22–23; Ephesians 1:13.

BLOCK 2: STORY PAGE (Real Life Scenario)

Story Title: The Worst Tuesday Ever   **Setting:** The car ride home after school.

The Story Liam slammed the car door and slumped against the window. It had been a terrible Tuesday. First, he forgot his homework. Then, during recess, his best friend ignored him to play with the cool kids. To top it off, he tripped in the hallway, and two fourth graders laughed.

"Rough day?" Mom asked, looking in the rearview mirror. "The worst," Liam mumbled. "I just want to go to bed and never come out." He felt small, lonely, and heavy, like he was carrying a backpack full of rocks. Mom sighed sympathetically. "I've had days like that. It feels awful to feel alone." "I *am* alone," Liam said. "Actually," Mom said gently, "you aren't. Remember what we talked about Sunday? When you belong to Jesus, who is with you, even in the backseat of a minivan on a bad Tuesday?"

The Choice Liam stared out the window. He could keep sulking and believe the lie that no one cared. Or he could remember that God wasn't just far away in heaven, He was right there.

Resolution Liam took a deep breath. "The Holy Spirit?" he asked quietly. "Right," Mom said. "He's the Helper. You can talk to Him right now and ask for peace." Liam closed his eyes. The bad day didn't magically disappear, but as he whispered a short prayer, the "heavy backpack" feeling started to lift just a little. He wasn't alone.

Takeaway Even on our worst days, the Holy Spirit is the Helper who is always with us to comfort us.

BLOCK 3: TALK-IT-OUT (Discussion + Coaching)

1. **Understand:** Who is the Holy Spirit, is He a power (like electricity) or a Person? (Hint: He is a Person, fully God!)

2. **Connect:** In the story, how did remembering the Holy Spirit help Liam?

3. **Apply:** What is one thing you need help with this week (fear, homework, being kind)? How can you ask the Spirit for help?

If your kid says: "Is the Holy Spirit a ghost?" **Try:** "No, the word 'Ghost' here just means 'Spirit' or 'Breath' in old language. He isn't a spooky ghost like in cartoons; He is the invisible presence of God."

If your kid says: "I don't feel Him inside me." **Try:** "That's normal. We don't always *feel* our heartbeat, but it's keeping us alive. The Spirit works quietly, giving us love for God and helping us fight sin, whether we feel goosebumps or not."

BLOCK 4: PRACTICE (One Habit This Week)

One Habit: The "Help!" Prayer The Holy Spirit loves to answer the shortest prayer in the world: "Help!"

When we'll do it: Pick one hard moment this week, a math test, a scary dark room, or when you're angry.

What to watch for: See if your heart calms down or if you remember a Bible verse. That's the Spirit working!

Prayer Holy Spirit, thank You for being my Helper. I am glad I am not alone. Please help me love Jesus more today. Amen.

BLOCK 5: PARENT NOTES (The Secret Weapon)

The Doctrine: The Holy Spirit The Holy Spirit is the third Person of the Trinity. He is fully God, co-eternal with the Father and the Son. He is not an "it" or a generic "force" like gravity. Jesus describes Him as a Person who speaks, teaches, grieves, and comforts. His main job is to shine a spotlight on Jesus, making our hearts come alive to trust Christ and empowering us to live like Him.

Why It Matters

- **Assurance:** We aren't left to live the Christian life on our own power.

- **Intimacy:** God isn't just "up there"; He is "in here."

- **Change:** We can't change our own hearts, but the Spirit can.

Common Misunderstanding to Avoid

- **Misunderstanding:** Thinking the Spirit is just a power source.

  ○ **Correction:** He is a Person we can know and talk to.

- **Misunderstanding:** Thinking the Spirit only shows up in wild, chaotic moments.

  ○ **Correction:** The Spirit is usually the author of peace, order, and self-control.

How to Answer Follow-Up Questions

- **Q: Why can't I see Him?**

  - A: "Just like you can't see the wind, but you see the trees move, you can't see the Spirit, but you see Him moving people to love and forgive."

- **Q: Does He ever leave?**

  - A: "Never. Jesus promised He would be with us forever."

Extra Bible anchors for parents John 14:16–17; Romans 8:9–11; Titus 3:5.

Christians Differ Box: Spiritual Gifts

What almost all Christians agree on:

- The Holy Spirit gives every believer gifts (abilities) to help the church (1 Corinthians 12).

- We should use these gifts to serve others, not to show off.

Common viewpoints:

- **Continuationist:** Believes all the gifts mentioned in the Bible (like healing, prophecy, and tongues) continue today and we should earnestly ask for them.

- **Cessationist:** Believes the "sign gifts" (like tongues and healing) were special miracles for the apostles to prove the Bible was true, so they don't happen the same way today.

- **Open but Cautious:** Believes miracles can happen, but we should be careful and test everything by Scripture.

How to be a good Christian about it: Even if Christians disagree on *which* gifts happen today, we all agree that the greatest evidence of the Spirit is **love** (1 Corinthians 13). We should respect other churches' views and ask our pastors for wisdom.

Teach-it-back prompt "If someone asked you, 'Who is the Helper?', what would you say?"

MEMORY (One-Liner + Catechism Q/A)

One-Line Definition The Holy Spirit is fully God, living inside believers to help us love and obey Jesus.

Q/A Q: Who is the Holy Spirit? **A:** He is the Third Person of the Trinity, our Helper and Comforter.

Notes:

WEEK 38: NEW BIRTH (REGENERATION)

<hr>

BLOCK 1: KID PAGE (Big Idea + Anchor Verse)

Big Idea We have a problem we can't fix on our own: our hearts naturally want to be the boss instead of God. We don't just need to try harder; we need to be made new. The Holy Spirit does a miracle called the "new birth", He takes out our stony, stubborn heart and gives us a soft heart that loves Jesus.

Anchor Verse *Ezekiel 36:26* **In kid words:** God promises to take away our heart of stone that is hard and stubborn, and give us a new, soft heart of flesh that wants to obey Him.

Key Words

- **Regeneration:** A big word for "being born again" or "made new."

- **Stone Heart:** A heart that is cold toward God and doesn't want to listen.

- **New Birth:** When the Holy Spirit wakes up our dead hearts to trust Jesus.

More Bible places to look: John 3:3–8; 2 Corinthians 5:17; Ephesians 2:4–5; Titus 3:5; 1 Peter 1:3.

BLOCK 2: STORY PAGE (Real Life Scenario)

Story Title: The Anger Snap   **Setting:** The living room, playing a video game.

The Story Whatever game they were playing, Maya was losing. "It's not fair! The controller is broken!" she yelled. Her little brother laughed. "No, you just missed the jump." Something hot bubbled up in Maya's chest. *Snap.* She threw the controller on the ground. Plastic cracked. The room went silent. Later, in her room, Maya cried. She had promised herself, and her parents, that she wouldn't blow up like that anymore. She tried to be nice. She tried to count to ten. But the anger was always there, waiting to explode. "I can't stop it," she told her dad later. "I try to be good, but inside, I'm just... mean."

The Choice Maya could make more promises to "try harder next time," or she could admit that her "try-harder" button was broken.

Resolution Dad sat on the edge of the bed. "Maya, trying to fix your own heart is like trying to do surgery on yourself, you just can't do it alone. That's why we need Jesus to give us a new one." Maya wiped her eyes. "So I need a new heart?" "Exactly," Dad said. "And that's exactly what the Holy Spirit gives us. He changes us from the inside out."

Takeaway We can't fix our sin by just trying harder; we need the Holy Spirit to give us a new heart.

BLOCK 3: TALK-IT-OUT (Discussion + Coaching)

1. **Understand:** What is the difference between a "heart of stone" and a "heart of flesh"?

2. **Connect:** Have you ever promised to stop doing something (lying, hitting, yelling) but then did it again? How did that feel?

3. **Apply:** Instead of just saying "I'll do better," what can we ask God to do for our hearts?

If your kid says: "Am I born again?" **Try:** "That is the most important question ever. Do you trust Jesus to save you? Do you want to follow Him, even imperfectly? Those are signs that the Spirit has given you a new heart."

If your kid says: "I still sin, so maybe I don't have a new heart." **Try:** "Having a new heart doesn't mean we are perfect yet. It means we *care* when we sin and want to turn back to Jesus. A stone heart wouldn't care at all."

BLOCK 4: PRACTICE (One Habit This Week)

One Habit: The "Make Me New" Prayer We need God's power every day, not just once.

When we'll do it: Every morning before breakfast.

What to watch for: Notice if you feel a little softer toward your siblings or parents today.

Prayer God, thank You for taking out my heart of stone. Please soften my heart today. Help me love what You love. Amen.

BLOCK 5: PARENT NOTES (The Secret Weapon)

The Doctrine: Regeneration (New Birth) Regeneration is the secret, sovereign work of the Holy Spirit where He imparts spiritual life to a spiritually dead sinner. Before this happens, we are "dead in trespasses" (Ephesians 2:1), we might be moral, but we have no true appetite for God. We cannot reason, work, or educate ourselves into the Kingdom. We must be "born again" (John 3). This is a one-time event that starts the lifelong process of growth.

Why It Matters

- **Humility:** We take zero credit for our salvation. It is God's gift.

- **Hope:** No one is "too far gone." If God can raise the dead, He can save anyone.

- **Relief:** Parenting isn't about behavior modification; it's about praying for heart transformation.

Common Misunderstanding to Avoid

- **Misunderstanding:** Thinking we start the Christian life by trying really hard.

  ○ **Correction:** Dead people can't try. God makes us alive first.

- **Misunderstanding:** Thinking "born again" people never sin.

  ○ **Correction:** New birth starts the war against sin; it doesn't end it instantly.

How to Answer Follow-Up Questions

- **Q: How does the new birth happen?**

  - A: "Usually, it happens when we hear the good news about Jesus. The Spirit uses the Bible to wake up our hearts so we say, 'Yes! I believe that!'"

- **Q: Can I be born again twice?**

  - A: "No, just like you were born physically once, you are born spiritually once. God doesn't un-adopt His children."

Extra Bible anchors for parents John 1:12–13; James 1:18; 1 Peter 1:23.

Teach-it-back prompt "Why did Maya in the story need more than just 'trying harder'?"

MEMORY (One-Liner + Catechism Q/A)

One-Line Definition New Birth is the miracle where God replaces our hard heart with a soft heart that loves Him.

Q/A Q: Can we change our own hearts? **A:** No, only the Holy Spirit can give us a new heart.

Notes:

WEEK 39: SANCTIFICATION

BLOCK 1: KID PAGE (Big Idea + Anchor Verse)

Big Idea God saves us instantly, but He changes us gradually. This process is called Sanctification, and it is like a tree growing slowly over time to produce fruit. It takes a whole lifetime, and the Holy Spirit helps us every step of the way.

Anchor Verse *Philippians 1:6* **In kid words:** I am sure of this: God, who started a good work in you, will keep working on it until the day Jesus comes back.

Key Words

- **Sanctification:** A big word meaning "being made holy" or "growing like Jesus."

- **Holy:** Set apart for God; pure and good.

- **Progress:** Moving forward, even if it's slow.

More Bible places to look: Romans 8:29; 2 Corinthians 3:18; Galatians 5:16; 1 Thessalonians 4:3; 2 Peter 3:18.

BLOCK 2: STORY PAGE (Real Life Scenario)

Story Title: The Tomato Plant   **Setting:** The backyard garden.

The Story Samir stared at the small green sprout in the dirt. "It's doing nothing," he complained. "I planted the seeds two days ago. I watered it. I put it in the sun. Where are the tomatoes?" His dad laughed. "Samir, you can't force a plant to grow instantly. It takes all summer." Samir sighed. "I hate waiting. I want to be a better Christian *now*, too. Yesterday I lied about brushing my teeth, and today I was mean to my sister. I thought asking Jesus into my heart would fix all that instantly." Dad knelt down beside the tiny plant. "Being a Christian is a lot like gardening. You are alive, that's the sprout. But growing tall and strong? That takes time, sun, water, and weeding."

The Choice Samir could give up because he wasn't perfect yet, or he could trust that God was growing him slowly.

Resolution "So God isn't mad that I'm not a giant tree yet?" Samir asked. "No," Dad said. "He's the Gardener. He's happy to watch you grow, leaf by leaf."

Takeaway Growing to be like Jesus takes time, just like a plant growing in a garden.

BLOCK 3: TALK-IT-OUT (Discussion + Coaching)

1. **Understand:** Does God fix everything about us the second we believe, or does it take time?

2. **Connect:** Is there something you are struggling to stop doing? Does it feel like it's taking a long time to change?

3. **Apply:** What is one "weed" (sin) you and the Holy Spirit can work on pulling up this week?

If your kid says: "I keep messing up. Maybe I'm not a Christian." **Try:** "The fact that it bothers you is a great sign! If you weren't a Christian, you wouldn't care. Fighting sin is proof of life."

If your kid says: "Why doesn't God just zap me perfect?" **Try:** "He could, but He loves to teach us to trust Him. Growing makes our relationship with Him stronger."

BLOCK 4: PRACTICE (One Habit This Week)

One Habit: The "Not Yet" Celebration When you make a mistake, don't hide. Confess it, then say: "God is not finished with me yet!"

When we'll do it: Whenever we mess up this week.

What to watch for: See if this helps you feel hope instead of shame.

Prayer Lord Jesus, thank You for saving me. Thank You for changing me. Be patient with me while I grow. Make me more like You. Amen.

BLOCK 5: PARENT NOTES (The Secret Weapon)

The Doctrine: Sanctification Sanctification is the progressive work of God and man that makes us more and more free from sin and like Christ in our actual lives.

- **Justification** is a one-time legal verdict (Position).

- **Sanctification** is a lifelong process of growth (Condition). We participate in this (by obeying, reading Scripture, praying), but the power comes entirely from the Spirit.

Why It Matters

- **Patience:** We learn to be patient with ourselves and our children.

- **Effort:** It explains why the Christian life feels like a fight. We are battling the "old self."

- **Hope:** We know we aren't stuck this way forever.

Common Misunderstanding to Avoid

- **Misunderstanding:** The "Let Go and Let God" Error: Thinking we do nothing.

  - **Correction:** The Bible tells us to "flee," "fight," and "run." We strive with His strength.

- **Misunderstanding:** The "Instant Zap" Error: Expecting instant maturity.

  - **Correction:** Fruit takes a season to grow.

How to Answer Follow-Up Questions

- **Q: Will I ever be perfect?**

  - A: "Not in this life. But when Jesus comes back, He will finish the work and make us perfect forever."

- **Q: Does God like me when I'm struggling?**

  - A: "Yes! He loves you because you are His child, not because of how well you performed today."

Extra Bible anchors for parents Romans 6:19; Hebrews 12:14; 1 Thessalonians 5:23.

Teach-it-back prompt "How is growing in faith like growing a tomato plant?"

MEMORY (One-Liner + Catechism Q/A)

One-Line Definition Sanctification is the lifelong process of the Holy Spirit making us more like Jesus.

Q/A Q: Are Christians perfect right away? **A:** No, we grow slowly, like a tree, until we meet Jesus.

Notes:

WEEK 40: SPIRITUAL PRACTICES

BLOCK 1: KID PAGE (Big Idea + Anchor Verse)

Big Idea God gives us special tools like prayer and Bible reading to help our faith grow strong. We call these "Spiritual Practices," and they act like healthy food for our souls. We don't do them to earn God's love, but to get close to Him and receive His power.

Anchor Verse *1 Timothy 4:7–8* **In kid words:** Do not waste time on silly myths. Instead, train yourself to be godly, like an athlete trains for a race.

Key Words

- **Spiritual Practices:** Habits (like prayer and Bible reading) that help us know God better.

- **Training:** Doing something over and over so you get stronger at it.

- **Means of Grace:** A fancy phrase meaning "ways God gives us strength."

More Bible places to look: Psalm 1:1–3; Psalm 119:9–11; Matthew 6:6; Acts 2:42; Colossians 3:16.

BLOCK 2: STORY PAGE (Real Life Scenario)

Story Title: The Dusty Bible   **Setting:** Bedroom, Sunday night.

The Story Jada looked at her Bible on the nightstand. It had a thin layer of dust on it. She hadn't opened it since last Sunday. "I'm terrible at this," she thought. "I promised I'd read five minutes a day." She felt guilty. It felt easier to just ignore it than to admit she had failed. She started to put a comic book on top of the Bible so she wouldn't have to look at it. Dad knocked on the door. "Hey, Jada. Everything okay?" "No," Jada admitted. "I'm bad at being a Christian. I keep forgetting to read my Bible." Dad sat down. "Jada, imagine if you forgot to eat breakfast and lunch. Would you say, 'I'm bad at eating, so I'll just starve'?" "No! I'd be super hungry. I'd go eat right now." "Exactly," Dad smiled. "The Bible is food for your soul. If you miss a few days, don't feel guilty. Just eat."

The Choice Jada could let guilt keep her away from God, or she could simply pick up the Bible and "eat."

Resolution Jada wiped the dust off the cover. She opened to a Psalm. It wasn't a chore; it was a meal. And she was hungry.

Takeaway Spiritual habits aren't about earning points; they are about feeding our souls so we can grow.

BLOCK 3: TALK-IT-OUT (Discussion + Coaching)

1. **Understand:** Why did Jada's dad compare the Bible to food?

2. **Connect:** Do you ever feel like reading the Bible or praying is a boring chore? Why?

3. **Apply:** What is one small habit we can start this week? (Start small: 3 minutes a day!)

If your kid says: "It's boring." **Try:** "Sometimes eating vegetables is boring, but they make you strong. And the more you read the Bible, the more you start to love the taste of it."

If your kid says: "I don't have time." **Try:** "We always make time for what we love (like TV or games). Let's try doing it first thing in the morning before the day gets busy."

BLOCK 4: PRACTICE (One Habit This Week)

One Habit: The 5-Minute Meeting Set a timer for 5 minutes. Read one short Psalm (like Psalm 23 or Psalm 100) and pray about it. That's it!

When we'll do it: Before school or right before bed.

What to watch for: Notice if your day feels different when you start with God.

Prayer God, thank You for giving us the Bible and prayer. Help me not to see them as chores, but as ways to be with You. Train me to be strong. Amen.

BLOCK 5: PARENT NOTES (The Secret Weapon)

The Doctrine: Means of Grace God has ordained specific channels through which He pours His grace into our lives. The primary ones are the Word (Scripture), Prayer, and Fellowship (Church/Sacraments). We don't do these to *earn* salvation, but to *enjoy* and *rest* in it. Just as we must eat and sleep to maintain physical life, we must use these means to maintain spiritual vigor.

Why It Matters

- **Power:** We can't grow by willpower alone. We need to plug into the power source.

- **Routine:** Faith isn't just a feeling; it's a lifestyle of holy habits.

- **Accessibility:** God hasn't made spiritual growth a mystery. He's told us exactly how to do it.

Common Misunderstanding to Avoid

- **Misunderstanding:** The "Checklist" Error: Thinking God loves us more because we ticked the boxes.

  - **Correction:** We are loved because of Jesus. We read to enjoy that love.

- **Misunderstanding:** The "Legalism" Fear: Afraid to enforce routines because it feels forced.

  - **Correction:** Discipline creates room for delight. Piano players practice scales so they can play beautiful music.

How to Answer Follow-Up Questions

- **Q: What if I don't feel anything when I pray?**

    ○ A: "That's okay. When you eat a sandwich, you don't always feel excitement, but it still nourishes your body. Prayer nourishes your spirit even when it feels ordinary."

- **Q: Do I have to do it every day?**

    ○ A: "It's good to! But if you miss a day, God isn't mad. Just pick it back up, like getting back on a bike."

Extra Bible anchors for parents Joshua 1:8; Matthew 6:5–13; Hebrews 4:16.

Teach-it-back prompt "Why did we compare reading the Bible to eating lunch?"

MEMORY (One-Liner + Catechism Q/A)

One-Line Definition Spiritual practices are habits like Bible reading and prayer that connect us to God's power.

Q/A Q: Why do we practice spiritual habits? **A:** To train our hearts to love God, just like an athlete trains for a race.

Notes:

WEEK 41: BAPTISM & WHAT IT MEANS

BLOCK 1: KID PAGE (Big Idea + Anchor Verse)

Big Idea Baptism is a special ceremony Jesus gave the church to show a picture of what He did for us. Going under the water shows we are buried with Him, and coming up shows we are raised to new life. It is like a wedding ring that tells the whole world we belong to Jesus.

Anchor Verse *Matthew 28:19* **In kid words:** Jesus told His followers to go and make disciples of all nations, baptizing them in the name of the Father, the Son, and the Holy Spirit.

Key Words

- **Baptism:** Using water to mark someone as a follower of Jesus.

- **Symbol:** Something we see (like a ring or flag) that stands for something invisible (like love or a country).

- **Ordinance/Sacrament:** A special practice Jesus commanded the church to do.

More Bible places to look: Acts 2:38; Acts 8:36–38; Romans 6:3–4; Galatians 3:27; Colossians 2:12.

BLOCK 2: STORY PAGE (Real Life Scenario)

Story Title: Watching from the Pew   **Setting:** Sunday morning church service.

The Story Caleb sat on the edge of the pew. Up front, the pastor was standing in the baptismal pool. A teenager named Marcus was standing there, looking nervous but happy. "I baptize you in the name of the Father, the Son, and the Holy Spirit," the pastor said. *Splash!* Marcus went under the water and came up soaking wet, grinning. Everyone clapped. "Does the water wash his sins away?" Caleb whispered to his dad. "Like a bath?" Dad whispered back, "No, the water is just regular water. It's a picture. Jesus already washed Marcus's sins away when he trusted in Him. This is Marcus's way of wearing the team jersey."

The Choice Caleb watched Marcus dry off. He realized baptism wasn't magic, it was a message.

Resolution "I want to wear the jersey someday," Caleb thought. "I want everyone to know I'm on Jesus' team."

Takeaway Baptism doesn't save us, but it shows the world that we belong to Jesus.

<u>BLOCK 3: TALK-IT-OUT (Discussion + Coaching)</u>

1. **Understand:** Does baptism wash away our sins, or is it a picture of something that already happened?

2. **Connect:** Why is it important to do things "in public" (like wearing a wedding ring or getting baptized) instead of keeping it a secret?

3. **Apply:** Have you been baptized? If not, is that something you are thinking about? (Parents: Use this to talk about your church's timing).

If your kid says: "I want to get baptized right now!" **Try:** "That is awesome! Let's talk to our pastor about what that means and when the right time is."

If your kid says: "I'm scared of going underwater." **Try:** "That's a normal fear. But remember, the pastor is holding you, and it only lasts one second. The joy is much bigger than the fear."

<u>BLOCK 4: PRACTICE (One Habit This Week)</u>

One Habit: Remember Your Baptism (or Look Forward to It) If you are baptized, find a photo or date of it. If not, pray about your future baptism.

When we'll do it: At dinner one night.

What to watch for: Talk about whose "team" you are on.

Prayer Jesus, thank You for washing away my sins. Thank You for the gift of baptism to show the world that I belong to You. Amen.

<u>BLOCK 5: PARENT NOTES (The Secret Weapon)</u>

The Doctrine: Baptism Baptism is the initiation rite of the Christian church. It signifies our union with Christ in His death and resurrection (Romans 6), the washing away of sins, and our entry into the covenant community. It is a visible word, God's promise seen with our eyes.

If your kid says:

- **Public Profession:** It is the "going public" moment of faith.

- **Identity:** It marks us as distinct from the world.

- **Unity:** It connects us to Christians all over the world and throughout history.

Common Misunderstanding to Avoid

- **Misunderstanding:** The "Magic Water" Error: Thinking the act itself saves a person.

  ○ **Correction:** We are saved by grace through faith. Baptism is the sign of that faith.

- **Misunderstanding:** The "Private Christian" Error: Thinking we can follow Jesus without identifying with His church.

  ○ **Correction:** Jesus commanded baptism; it's not optional for obedience.

How to Answer Follow-Up Questions

- **Q: Why do we do it?**

  - A: "Because Jesus told us to, and because He did it too! It's our way of saying, 'I'm with Him.'"

- **Q: Can I get baptized again?**

  - A: (Depends on tradition, but generally): "Usually, baptism is a one-time thing because it marks the start of your journey."

Extra Bible anchors for parents Mark 16:16; Acts 22:16; 1 Peter 3:21.

Christians Differ Box: Baptism

What almost all Christians agree on:

- Baptism is important and commanded by Jesus.

- It involves water and the name of the Trinity (Father, Son, Holy Spirit).

- It is a sign of God's grace and our cleansing from sin.

Common viewpoints:

- **Credobaptism (Believer's Baptism):** believes only people who are old enough to profess faith should be baptized. They usually immerse (dunk) the person. (Baptists, Non-denominational).

- **Paedobaptism (Infant Baptism):** believes children of believers should be baptized as a sign of entering God's covenant family, just like boys in the Old Testament were circumcised. They usually sprinkle or pour water. (Presbyterians, Anglicans, Lutherans, Methodists).

How to be a good Christian about it: We should not fight over the water! Whether your church sprinkles babies or dunks adults, both sides love Jesus and want to obey the Bible. Follow the leadership of your church and respect friends who do it differently.

Teach-it-back prompt "What did Caleb's dad say baptism is like? (Hint: A team jersey)."

MEMORY (One-Liner + Catechism Q/A)

One-Line Definition Baptism is the sign that marks us as members of God's family.

Q/A Q: What does baptism show the world? **A:** That we have been washed from sin and now belong to Jesus.

Notes:

WEEK 42: THE LORD'S SUPPER (COMMUNION)

BLOCK 1: KID PAGE (Big Idea + Anchor Verse)

Big Idea The night before Jesus died, He ate a special meal with His disciples. He gave them bread and a cup and said, "Do this in remembrance of me." Today, the church eats this meal to look back at Jesus' death (the bread is His body, the cup is His blood) and to look forward to the day we will eat with Him in heaven. It nourishes our faith.

Anchor Verse *1 Corinthians 11:26* **In kid words:** Every time you eat this bread and drink this cup, you are telling the story of the Lord's death until He comes back.

Key Words

- **Communion:** A word meaning "sharing" or "fellowship." We share the meal with Jesus and each other.

- **Remembrance:** Thinking deeply about something so you don't forget.

- **The Lord's Supper:** Another name for Communion.

More Bible places to look: Matthew 26:26–29; Luke 22:19–20; 1 Corinthians 10:16–17.

BLOCK 2: STORY PAGE (Real Life Scenario)

Story Title: The Tiny Cup   **Setting:** Church, holding the communion tray.

The Story The shiny silver tray came down the row. It was full of tiny cups of juice. Behind it was a plate of crackers. Ava reached out her hand. "I'm hungry," she whispered. Her dad gently caught her hand. "Not yet, sweetie." "But why?" Ava whispered back. "It's just a cracker." Dad leaned in close. "It's not a snack. It's a special meal for family members. When we eat this, we are saying, 'Jesus' body was broken for me.' It's a very serious and happy promise. We have to understand it before we eat it." Ava pulled her hand back. She watched her dad eat and drink with his eyes closed, looking grateful.

The Choice Ava could be mad she didn't get a snack, or she could wonder, "What makes that little cracker so special?"

Resolution "I want to understand," Ava whispered. "I know," Dad smiled. "And when you're ready to trust Jesus and understand the promise, we will celebrate your first communion together."

Takeaway Communion isn't a snack; it's a holy meal where Christians remember Jesus' sacrifice.

BLOCK 3: TALK-IT-OUT (Discussion + Coaching)

1. **Understand:** What do the bread and the cup stand for?

2. **Connect:** Why did Ava's dad say she should wait? Was he being mean or protecting her?

3. **Apply:** (Parents, explain your church's view on when kids partake). What do you think about when you see people taking communion?

If your kid says: "Can I have some?" **Try:** "This is a family meal for those who have trusted Jesus. Let's talk to our pastor about when you will be ready to join in."

If your kid says: "It tastes weird." **Try:** "It's not meant to fill our tummies or taste like candy. It's meant to fill our hearts with thanks for Jesus."

BLOCK 4: PRACTICE (One Habit This Week)

One Habit: The "Thank You" Meal At dinner one night, before you eat, take a moment to say, "Thank You, Jesus, for Your body and blood."

When we'll do it: Tonight at dinner.

What to watch for: Remember that Jesus is the real food for our souls.

Prayer Lord Jesus, thank You that Your body was broken and Your blood was shed for me. Prepare my heart to come to Your table with joy. Amen.

BLOCK 5: PARENT NOTES (The Secret Weapon)

The Doctrine: The Lord's Supper Communion is the ongoing sign of the New Covenant. While baptism happens once (entry), communion happens repeatedly (renewal). It is a time of looking back (to the Cross), looking around (at the Body of Christ/church unity), and looking forward (to the Marriage Supper of the Lamb). It spiritually nourishes believers.

Why It Matters

- **Tangible:** God knows we are forgetful humans who need physical reminders (taste, touch) of spiritual truths.

- **Proclamation:** It is a sermon without words. We "proclaim the Lord's death" (1 Cor 11:26).

- **Self-Examination:** It creates a regular rhythm of confessing sin and realigning our hearts.

Common Misunderstanding to Avoid

- **Misunderstanding:** The "Snack" Error: Treating it casually or irreverently.

  - **Correction:** Paul warns us to discern the body and eat worthily.

- **Misunderstanding:** The "Superstition" Error: Thinking the bread itself has magical healing powers.

  - **Correction:** It is faith in Christ that heals and saves.

How to Answer Follow-Up Questions

- **Q: Why do we do it so often?**

  - A: "Because we are forgetful! We need to be reminded constantly that Jesus loves us and died for us."

- **Q: Who is allowed to eat it?**

  - A: "Anyone who has turned from their sin and trusted Jesus as their King. It's the family meal for Christians."

Extra Bible anchors for parents Acts 2:42; 1 Corinthians 10:16; 1 Corinthians 11:23–29.

Christians Differ Box: Communion

What almost all Christians agree on:

- Jesus commanded us to observe this supper.

- The bread represents His body; the cup represents His blood.

- It is a holy moment of worship and thanksgiving (Eucharist).

Common viewpoints:

- **Memorial View:** The bread and juice are symbols to help us *remember* Jesus. Jesus is present in our hearts, not the bread. (Many Baptists/Non-denominational).

- **Spiritual Presence:** Jesus is spiritually present in a special way when we eat. By faith, we are nourished by Him. (Presbyterians/Reformed).

- **Physical Presence:** The elements actually become or contain the body and blood of Christ in a mystery. (Lutherans, Catholics, Orthodox).

How to be a good Christian about it: We approach the table with reverence. Even if we explain the "how" differently, we all agree on the "Who." We are there to meet with Jesus.

Teach-it-back prompt "What are the two things the bread and cup stand for?"

MEMORY (One-Liner + Catechism Q/A)

One-Line Definition Communion is the family meal where we remember that Jesus died for us.

Q/A Q: Why do we eat the bread and drink the cup? **A:** To proclaim the Lord's death until He comes back.

Notes:

WEEK 43: REVIEW: GROWING UP IN JESUS

BLOCK 1: KID PAGE (Big Idea + Anchor Verse)

Big Idea Being a Christian isn't just about a one-time decision; it is about growing up in faith. Just like you grow out of your shoes, your trust in Jesus should grow bigger and stronger every year. The Holy Spirit is the one who makes this happen by changing us from the inside out.

Anchor Verse *2 Peter 3:18* **In kid words:** Keep growing in the grace and knowledge of our Lord and Savior Jesus Christ. All glory belongs to Him now and forever!

Key Words

- **Maturity:** Being fully grown up. In faith, it means loving and obeying Jesus more consistently.

- **Review:** Looking back at what we learned so we don't forget.

More Bible places to look: Ephesians 4:15; Colossians 1:10; Hebrews 6:1.

BLOCK 2: STORY PAGE (Real Life Scenario)

Story Title: The Shared Bedroom Line   **Setting:** A bedroom shared by two brothers, Ty and Leo.

The Story Ty took a roll of blue painter's tape and stuck it right down the middle of the floor. "This is my side," Ty said. "Stay out." Leo kicked a sock over the line. "Oops." "I'm telling!" Ty yelled. He was about to shove Leo when he stopped. He remembered the verse he learned last week about patience. He remembered asking the Holy Spirit for help. Ty took a deep breath. His hands were fists, but he didn't swing. "Leo, please move your sock," he said through gritted teeth. Leo looked surprised. "Okay." Later, Mom said, "Ty, I saw that. Last year, you would have hit him. You're changing." Ty looked at his hands. "It was hard. But I felt... checked. Like someone tapped me on the shoulder to stop."

The Choice Ty could have acted like his old self, or he could listen to the new nudge of the Spirit.

Resolution "That's the Holy Spirit," Mom said. "He's growing you up."

Takeaway Growth happens when we listen to the Holy Spirit in the hard moments.

BLOCK 3: TALK-IT-OUT (Discussion + Coaching)

1. **Understand:** Did Ty become perfect instantly? (No, he was still mad, but he controlled it).

2. **Connect:** Look back at the last year. Is there a way you have grown? (Are you kinder? Do you pray more?)

3. **Apply:** What is one area you still feel "little" in and want to grow up? (Maybe sharing, telling the truth, or not whining).

If your kid says: "I haven't grown at all." **Try:** "Ask people who love you. Sometimes we can't see our own growth, just like you don't feel yourself getting taller. But I see changes in you!"

If your kid says: "Is God mad that I'm slow?" **Try:** "Never. He is a patient Father. He loves watching you take baby steps."

BLOCK 4: PRACTICE (One Habit This Week)

One Habit: The Growth Chart Draw a simple tree on a paper. Write one "fruit" on it that you have seen lately (like Patience or Kindness).

When we'll do it: During art time or after dinner.

What to watch for: Thank God for making the fruit grow. You didn't do it alone!

Prayer Holy Spirit, thank You for working in my heart. Thank You that I am not the same as I was last year. Keep growing me until I look like Jesus. Amen.

BLOCK 5: PARENT NOTES (The Secret Weapon)

The Doctrine: Spiritual Growth (Progressive Sanctification) This week is a review week. We are consolidating the truths that the Christian life is dynamic, not static. We are saved by grace (Monergism, God's work alone), but we grow through a relationship where we respond and act (Synergism, we work because He works).

Why It Matters

- **Encouragement:** It helps kids see that small victories count.

- **Trajectory:** It sets the expectation that life is a journey, not a destination we reach at age 10.

Common Misunderstanding to Avoid

- **Misunderstanding:** The "Behaviorism" Trap: Focusing only on outside actions.

  - **Correction:** Ty didn't just not hit; he fought an internal battle with the Spirit's help.

- **Misunderstanding:** The "Stagnation" Trap: thinking it's okay to stay a baby Christian forever.

  - **Correction:** We are commanded to grow.

How to Answer Follow-Up Questions

- **Q: Why is growing so hard?**

  - A: "Because our old sinful nature fights back. It's like swimming upstream. But the Spirit is stronger than the current."

- **Q: How do I grow faster?**

  - A: "Stay close to the sunlight (Jesus) and drink plenty of water (Bible). Growth happens naturally when you stay close to Him."

Extra Bible anchors for parents Colossians 2:6–7; 2 Peter 1:5–8; Ephesians 4:15.

Teach-it-back prompt "What is one way you have seen our family grow in faith this year?"

MEMORY (One-Liner + Catechism Q/A)

One-Line Definition Spiritual growth means trusting Jesus more today than we did yesterday.

Q/A Q: Who causes us to grow in faith? **A:** The Holy Spirit works in us to make us like Christ.

Notes:

WEEK 44: LIFE SKILL: TEMPTATION & SPIRITUAL BATTLE

BLOCK 1: KID PAGE (Big Idea + Anchor Verse)

Big Idea Even though we have new hearts, enemies like the devil and our own bad desires still try to trick us into sinning. Being tempted isn't a sin, but saying "yes" to the temptation is. The good news is that God is faithful and always provides a way of escape so we can stand strong.

Anchor Verse *1 Corinthians 10:13* **In kid words:** You are not the only one who gets tempted. But God is faithful. He will not let you be tempted more than you can handle, and He will always make a way for you to escape so you can stand strong.

Key Words

- **Temptation:** A lie that tries to trick you into disobeying God.

- **The Flesh:** The part of us that still wants to be selfish.

- **Escape Route:** The way out that God provides when we are tempted.

More Bible places to look: Matthew 4:1–11; James 1:13–15; James 4:7; 1 Peter 5:8; Ephesians 6:11.

BLOCK 2: STORY PAGE (Real Life Scenario)

Story Title: The Cheat Sheet   **Setting:** The classroom, during a big spelling test.

The Story Ben hadn't studied. He stared at his blank paper. His palms were sweaty. Right next to him, Chloe had her paper wide open. Ben could see every answer. The thought hit him *woosh*: "Just look. It's easy. Everyone does it. You need an A." It felt like a magnet pulling his eyes toward Chloe's desk. Ben remembered the verse from Sunday: *God always provides a way of escape.* He looked around, desperate for that way out. The teacher turned her back. This was the moment. Ben squeezed his pencil. "God, help me," he whispered. Suddenly, he had an idea. He covered his eyes with his hand and looked straight down at his own desk. He guessed on the answers, but he didn't look.

The Choice Ben could take the easy A and a guilty conscience, or a bad grade and a clean heart.

Resolution Ben got a C-minus. But when he walked out of class, he felt light as a feather. He had won the battle.

Takeaway When temptation pulls you toward sin, look for the "Escape Route" God promises.

BLOCK 3: TALK-IT-OUT (Discussion + Coaching)

1. **Understand:** Was it a sin for Ben to *feel* like looking? (No, that was the temptation. The sin would be looking).

2. **Connect:** What are the things that tempt you the most? (Lying to get out of trouble? Taking things? Being mean to look cool?)

3. **Apply:** What is an "Escape Route" you can use? (Walk away? Close your eyes? Say a Bible verse out loud?)

If your kid says: "The devil made me do it." **Try:** "The devil can tempt you, but he can't make your muscles move. You made the choice. We have to own our sin."

If your kid says: "It's too hard to resist." **Try:** "It feels hard, but God promises in 1 Corinthians 10:13 that it's never impossible. He always gives strength if we ask."

BLOCK 4: PRACTICE (One Habit This Week)

One Habit: The "Stop, Drop, and Pray" Just like fire safety! When you feel a temptation (to yell, to lie, to cheat):

1. **Stop** what you are doing.

2. **Drop** your head (or knees).

3. **Pray** "Jesus, show me the way out!" **When we'll do it:** In the heat of the moment. **What to watch for:** See how fast the temptation loses its power when you pray.

Prayer God, lead me not into temptation, but deliver me from evil. Give me eyes to see the escape route when I want to do wrong. Amen.

BLOCK 5: PARENT NOTES (The Secret Weapon)

The Doctrine: Spiritual Warfare & Temptation We are in a spiritual battle. We have three enemies:

1. **The World:** The system of values that opposes God.

2. **The Flesh:** Our own internal sinful desires.

3. **The Devil:** A real spiritual adversary who lies and deceives. However, "the one who is in you is greater than the one who is in the world" (1 John 4:4, CSB). Victory is possible through the Spirit.

Why It Matters

- **Awareness:** If kids don't know they are in a battle, they will be confused when they feel pulled to sin.

- **Confidence:** We don't fight *for* victory; we fight *from* victory. Jesus has already won.

Common Misunderstanding to Avoid

- **Misunderstanding:** The "Sin is Outside" Error: Thinking only "bad people" tempt us.

  - **Correction:** Our own hearts (the Flesh) tempt us too.

- **Misunderstanding:** The "Defeatist" Error: "I just can't help it."

  - **Correction:** As believers, we are no longer slaves to sin (Romans 6). We have a choice.

How to Answer Follow-Up Questions

- **Q: Why does God let us be tempted?**

    ◦ A: "It tests our faith and makes our muscles strong. Every time you say 'no' to sin, you get stronger for Jesus."

- **Q: Did Jesus really get tempted?**

    ◦ A: "Yes! The devil tried to get Him to disobey God, but Jesus used Scripture to fight back. He knows exactly how hard it feels."

Extra Bible anchors for parents Matthew 26:41; Hebrews 4:15; James 4:7.

Teach-it-back prompt "What is the difference between being *tempted* and *sinning*?"

MEMORY (One-Liner + Catechism Q/A)

One-Line Definition Temptation is an invitation to sin, but God always provides an escape route.

Q/A Q: What promise does God give about temptation? **A:** He promises that He will never let us be tempted beyond what we can bear (1 Corinthians 10:13).

Notes:

Part 6: Church & Hope

We finish the year the way God designed the Christian life to be lived: **together**, with our eyes on the end of the story. In this part we'll explore **community, mission, suffering, and the end times...** because loneliness is real, hardship is real, and kids need more than motivational quotes.

They need a family (the church) and a future (hope).

These weeks are meant to give your children belonging and backbone.

They'll learn they are not solo hikers trying to follow Jesus alone, and they're not stuck in a story that ends in darkness. We are headed somewhere.

And the ending is good, good enough to make the hard parts of life bearable, and strong enough to keep us faithful while we wait.

WEEK 45: THE CHURCH

BLOCK 1: KID PAGE (Big Idea + Anchor Verse)

Big Idea The Church is not a building made of bricks; it is a family made of people who trust Jesus. God never designed us to follow Him alone, like a lonely hiker. He gave us brothers and sisters to encourage us, correct us, and worship with us.

Anchor Verse *Hebrews 10:24–25* **In kid words:** Let us think of ways to encourage one another to love and do good deeds. Let us not stop meeting together, but let us encourage one another even more.

Key Words

- **The Body of Christ:** A name for the church showing that we all have different parts to play, just like hands and feet.

- **Gathering:** When the church meets together to worship and hear God's Word.

- **Communion of Saints:** The family connection between all Christians everywhere.

More Bible places to look: Acts 2:42–47; Romans 12:4–5; Ephesians 2:19–22; 1 Corinthians 12:12–27; Matthew 16:18.

BLOCK 2: STORY PAGE (Real Life Scenario)

Story Title: The Sunday Morning Drag **Setting:** Bedroom, Sunday morning, 8:15 AM.

The Story "Do I have to go?" Leo groaned, pulling the blanket over his head. "It's boring. The songs are long, and Mr. Henderson smells like old coffee." Dad pulled the blanket down. "Yup. We're going." Leo grumped all the way to the car. He slumped in the pew during the first song. But then, during the greeting time, Mr. Henderson, the coffee-smelling man, turned around. "Leo! How was that math test you were scared about?" he asked. Leo blinked. He didn't know Mr. Henderson remembered that. "I got a B," Leo said. "High five!" Mr. Henderson beamed. "I prayed for you on Tuesday morning." Leo sat back down. He looked around. It wasn't just a boring meeting. It was a room full of people who actually cared about him.

The Choice Leo could keep thinking church was a show to watch, or he could realize it was a family to belong to.

Resolution "Mr. Henderson is actually pretty cool," Leo told his dad on the ride home. "That's why we go," Dad said. "We need them, and they need us."

Takeaway Church isn't an event we watch; it's a family we belong to.

BLOCK 3: TALK-IT-OUT (Discussion + Coaching)

1. **Understand:** Is the church the building we sit in or the people we sit with?

2. **Connect:** What is the hardest part about going to church for you? (Getting up early? Sitting still? Not knowing anyone?)

3. **Apply:** Who is one person at church (besides our family) who encourages you? Let's thank God for them.

If your kid says: "Church is boring." **Try:** "Sometimes it feels that way. But we don't go to be entertained; we go to worship God and help others. It's not about what we *get*, but what we *give*."

If your kid says: "I can just worship God in my room." **Try:** "You can and should! But an ember from a fire goes cold if it sits alone. We stay hot by staying close to the other coals."

BLOCK 4: PRACTICE (One Habit This Week)

One Habit: The "Secret Encourager" Pick one person at church this Sunday (a pastor, a teacher, or a friend). Draw them a picture or write a note that says "Thanks for being part of my church family." Hand it to them.

When we'll do it: This Sunday morning.

What to watch for: See how much it makes them smile.

Prayer Jesus, thank You for the Church. Thank You that I have brothers and sisters to walk with. Help me to love Your family well. Amen.

BLOCK 5: PARENT NOTES (The Secret Weapon)

The Doctrine: Ecclesiology (The Church) The Church is the bride of Christ and the visible manifestation of His kingdom on earth. It is not an optional add-on to the Christian life; it is central to God's plan.

- **Universal Church:** All believers of all time.

- **Local Church:** A specific gathering of believers in a specific place with qualified leadership (elders/deacons) and the administration of the ordinances (baptism/communion).

Why it matters

- **Protection:** Sheep wandering alone get eaten by wolves. The church provides spiritual protection and oversight.

- **Growth:** We cannot practice the "one anothers" of Scripture (love one another, forgive one another) in isolation.

- **Worship:** Corporate worship aligns our hearts in a way private devotion cannot.

Common Misunderstanding to Avoid

- **Misunderstanding:** The "Consumer" Error: "I go to church to get fed."

  ○ **Correction**: We go to worship and serve. Maturity is feeding yourself and others.

- **Misunderstanding:** The "Hypocrite" Excuse: "The church is full of hypocrites."

  ○ **Correction**: Yes, it's a hospital for sinners, not a museum for saints. We fit right in.

How to Answer Follow-Up Questions

- **Q: Why are there so many different churches (Baptist, Methodist, etc.)?**

  - A: "Sometimes Christians disagree on smaller things like how to do baptism or church government. But if they love Jesus and believe the Bible, we are all on the same big team."

- **Q: What if I don't like the music?**

  - A: "That's a great chance to practice unselfishness! We sing to please God, not to be entertained."

Extra Bible anchors for parents Matthew 18:20; Acts 20:28; Ephesians 4:11–16; 1 Timothy 3:15.

Teach-it-back prompt "What is the difference between a building made of bricks and the Church?"

MEMORY (One-Liner + Catechism Q/A)

One-Line Definition The Church is God's family, gathered to worship Jesus and encourage one another.

Q/A Q: Is the church a building? **A:** No, the church is the people who belong to Jesus.

Notes:

WEEK 46: MISSION

BLOCK 1: KID PAGE (Big Idea + Anchor Verse)

Big Idea Before Jesus went back to heaven, He gave His followers a big job called the 'Great Commission.' It means we get to tell the world the good news about Jesus so they can join God's family too. We don't share this news because we are forced to, but because it is the best news in the world.

Anchor Verse *Matthew 28:19–20* **In kid words:** Go and make disciples of all nations, baptizing them and teaching them to obey everything I have commanded you. And remember, I am with you always.

Key Words

- **Evangelism:** Telling people the good news (Gospel) about Jesus.

- **Mission:** Being sent out to do a special job for God.

- **Witness:** Someone who simply tells what they have seen and heard.

More Bible places to look: Acts 1:8; Romans 10:13–15; 1 Peter 3:15; Mark 16:15; 2 Corinthians 5:20.

BLOCK 2: STORY PAGE (Real Life Scenario)

Story Title: The Empty Seat **Setting:** The school cafeteria.

The Story Maya sat with her tray. Across the table, Chloe looked sad. Chloe had been talking about how scared she was about her parents fighting. "I wish I had someone to talk to," Chloe mumbled. Maya's heart thumped. She knew she should invite Chloe to youth group. They were talking about peace this week. But what if Chloe said no? What if she thought Maya was weird? Maya took a bite of her sandwich to stall. *Be brave,* she thought. *You have good news.* "Hey," Maya said, her voice shaking a tiny bit. "My church has this fun group on Wednesdays. It really helps me when I'm scared. Do you want to come with me?" Chloe looked up. She didn't laugh. "Maybe," she said. "Thanks for asking."

The Choice Maya could keep her hope a secret to stay safe, or she could share it to help her friend.

Resolution Maya smiled. "I can save you a seat if you want." "Okay," Chloe said. "That would be nice."

Takeaway Sharing Jesus is just one beggar telling another beggar where to find bread.

BLOCK 3: TALK-IT-OUT (Discussion + Coaching)

1. **If your kid says: Understand:** What is the "job" Jesus gave us in the Anchor Verse?

2. **Connect:** Why was Maya scared to invite Chloe? Have you ever felt scared to talk about Jesus?

3. **Apply:** Who is one friend who doesn't know Jesus yet? Let's pray for them by name right now.

If your kid says: "I don't know enough to explain the Bible." **Try:** "You don't have to be a professor! You just have to say what you know. 'Jesus loves me and forgives me.' That is enough to start."

If your kid says: "What if they make fun of me?" **Try:** "They might. But Jesus said that's okay. It's an honor to be teased for being like Him. And you never know, they might be listening more than you think."

BLOCK 4: PRACTICE (One Habit This Week)

One Habit: The "Open Door" Prayer We can't force people to believe, but we can pray.

When we'll do it: On the way to school.

What to watch for: Pray: "Lord, give me a chance to show Your kindness to someone today." Then look for that chance!

Prayer Lord, thank You for saving me. Give me courage to share the Good News. Help me love my friends enough to tell them the truth. Amen.

BLOCK 5: PARENT NOTES (The Secret Weapon)

The Doctrine: Mission & Evangelism Mission flows from the heart of God. God is a sending God (He sent the Son; the Son sent the Spirit). Now, the Church is sent into the world. Evangelism isn't just a sales pitch; it's the overflow of our joy in Christ.

Why it matters

- **Love:** If we really believe the Gospel is true, the most unloving thing we can do is keep it to ourselves.

- **Purpose:** Kids need to know they aren't just on earth to get good grades and have fun; they are ambassadors for the King.

Common Misunderstanding to Avoid

- **Misunderstanding:** The "Professional" Error: Thinking only pastors engage in mission.

  ○ **Correction**: Every believer is a witness.

- **Misunderstanding:** The "Obnoxious" Error: Thinking mission means shouting at people.

  ○ **Correction**: We share with "gentleness and respect" (1 Peter 3:15).

How to Answer Follow-Up Questions

- **Q: What if I tell them about Jesus and they say no?**

    - A: "That is between them and God. Your job is just to deliver the mail, not to make them read it. You were successful just by sharing!"

- **Q: Do I have to go to another country to be a missionary?**

    - A: "Nope! Your mission field is your soccer team, your classroom, and our neighborhood. You are a missionary right now."

Extra Bible anchors for parents Isaiah 52:7; Matthew 5:14–16; Romans 1:16.

Teach-it-back prompt "What is the big job Jesus gave us before He went to heaven?"

MEMORY (One-Liner + Catechism Q/A)

One-Line Definition Mission is being sent by Jesus to tell the world the Good News.

Q/A Q: What is the Great Commission? **A:** Jesus' command to go and make disciples of all nations.

WEEK 47: SUFFERING & HOPE

BLOCK 1: KID PAGE (Big Idea + Anchor Verse)

Big Idea Sometimes life is really hard. People get sick, friends fight, and sad things happen. This can be scary, but it doesn't mean God has left us. The Bible teaches us that God is close to the brokenhearted. We have a "Living Hope" because Jesus suffered too, and He beat death. Because He lives, we know that sad stories don't last forever.

Anchor Verse *Romans 8:18* **In kid words:** I know that the suffering we feel right now is nothing compared to the glory God will show us later.

Key Words

- **Suffering:** Going through pain, sadness, or hard times.

- **Hope:** Not just "wishing" for something, but being *sure* that God keeps His promises.

- **Lament:** A special way of crying out to God when we are sad (like in the Psalms).

More Bible places to look: Psalm 34:18; John 16:33; 2 Corinthians 4:16–18; 1 Peter 1:3–6; Revelation 21:4.

BLOCK 2: STORY PAGE (Real Life Scenario)

Story Title: Voices Downstairs **Setting:** Top of the stairs, late at night.

The Story Sam woke up to voices. He crept to the landing. Mom and Dad were in the kitchen. "I don't know how we're going to pay for the car repair," Dad said, sounding tired. "And with Grandma getting sicker..." Mom's voice cracked. She was crying. Sam's stomach twisted into a knot. He thought grown-ups had everything figured out. If they were scared, who was going to take care of him? He hurried back to bed and pulled the covers up, shivering. The next morning, Sam dragged his feet. "Are we poor?" he asked at breakfast. Mom and Dad looked at each other. Dad pulled out a chair. "Come here, bud. We have some hard problems right now. But let me tell you who is bigger than our problems."

The Choice Sam could let the worry eat him up, or he could let his parents point him to the God who cares.

Resolution "We are sad, and we are praying," Dad said. "But we have hope. God has taken care of us before, and He isn't stopping now."

Takeaway Even when things are scary, we can trust that God is bigger than our problems.

BLOCK 3: TALK-IT-OUT (Discussion + Coaching)

1. **Understand:** Does being a Christian mean nothing bad will ever happen to us? (No, Jesus said we *would* have trouble).

2. **Connect:** When was the last time you felt really sad or worried? Did you talk to God about it?

3. **Apply:** What can we do as a family when we are going through a hard time? (Pray together, read Psalms, ask for help).

If your kid says: "Why did God let 'bad thing' happen?" **Try:** "That is a very big question. We live in a broken world because of sin. God doesn't cause evil, but He promises to use even the bad things for good in the end."

If your kid says: "I'm scared." **Try:** "It's okay to be scared. Even King David was scared. He wrote Psalm 56:3: 'When I am afraid, I put my trust in you.' Let's say that together."

BLOCK 4: PRACTICE (One Habit This Week)

One Habit: The "Lament" Drawing Take a piece of paper. On one side, draw/write what you are sad or worried about (broken toy, sick friend). On the other side, draw a Cross or a Sun to show God is there.

When we'll do it: If a sad moment happens, or just during quiet time.

What to watch for: Notice that you can give your heavy feelings to Jesus.

Prayer God, sometimes the world is sad and scary. Thank You that You are close to the brokenhearted. Thank You that because of Jesus, we have a hope that never ends. Amen.

BLOCK 5: PARENT NOTES (The Secret Weapon)

The Doctrine: Suffering & Providence Christianity does not deny the reality of suffering. Instead, it offers a framework for it. We suffer because of the Fall (general brokenness) and sometimes for righteousness' sake. But we believe in a Sovereign God who works all things together for good (Romans 8:28) and a future glory that outweighs present pain.

Why it matters

- **Realism:** Kids need to know that faith works in the dark, not just on sunny days.

- **Resilience:** A theology of suffering prevents a crisis of faith when the first bad thing happens.

Common Misunderstanding to Avoid

- **Misunderstanding:** The "Karma" Error: "Bad things happen because I was bad."

  ○ **Correction**: Job's friends thought this. Jesus corrected it (John 9). Suffering isn't always direct punishment.

- **Misunderstanding:** The "Stoic" Error: "Christians shouldn't cry."

  ○ **Correction**: Jesus wept. We grieve, but not as those without hope.

How to Answer Follow-Up Questions

- **Q: Does God care that I'm sad?**

    ◦ A: "Yes. He collects your tears in a bottle (Psalm 56). He feels your hurt."

- **Q: Will it be sad forever?**

    ◦ A: "No. The Bible promises a day when God will wipe away every tear from our eyes."

Extra Bible anchors for parents Job 19:25; Psalm 23; Romans 5:3–5; 1 Peter 4:12–13.

Teach-it-back prompt "Does being a Christian mean nothing sad will ever happen?"

MEMORY (One-Liner + Catechism Q/A)

One-Line Definition Christian hope is the sure confidence that God keeps His promises, even when life is hard.

Q/A Q: Why can we have hope in suffering? **A:** Because Jesus died and rose again to make all things new.

Notes:

WEEK 48: LAST THINGS: NEW CREATION

BLOCK 1: KID PAGE (Big Idea + Anchor Verse)

Big Idea The Bible story doesn't end with "The End." It ends with "A New Beginning." God isn't going to throw the world in the trash; He is going to fix it. He will make a New Heaven and a New Earth where there is no more sin, sickness, or sadness. We don't have to be afraid of the future because God wins!

Anchor Verse *Revelation 21:5* **In kid words:** The One sitting on the throne said, "Look! I am making everything new!"

Key Words

- **New Creation:** The future world where God fixes everything broken.

- **Restoration:** Making something old and broken look brand new again.

- **Glorification:** When our bodies and hearts are made perfect to live with God forever.

More Bible places to look: Isaiah 65:17; Romans 8:21; 2 Peter 3:13; Revelation 21:1–4; Revelation 22:1–5.

BLOCK 2: STORY PAGE (Real Life Scenario)

Story Title: The Speech Disaster **Setting:** School classroom, giving a presentation.

The Story Sophie held her index cards with shaky hands. She started to read her history report. "Abraham Lincoln was..." Then she sneezed. A loud, giant sneeze. Her index cards flew out of her hand and scattered all over the floor. The whole class laughed. Sophie turned bright red. She scrambled to pick them up, but she wanted to melt into the floor and disappear forever. That night, she buried her face in her pillow. "I'm never going back to school," she told her mom. "The shame is going to last forever." "It feels that way," Mom said, rubbing her back. "But shame is a liar. It doesn't last forever. Do you know what does?"

The Choice Sophie could believe her mistake defined her forever, or she could trust that God's future is bigger than her bad day.

Resolution "God promises a day when there will be no more crying, no more embarrassment, and no more mistakes," Mom said. "This bad day will pass. God's new world is coming."

Takeaway Our mistakes and sadness are temporary; God's renewal is forever.

BLOCK 3: TALK-IT-OUT (Discussion + Coaching)

1. **Understand:** Is God going to destroy the earth or renew it? (He will renew it/make it new).

2. **Connect:** Have you ever wished you could hit a "restart" button on a bad day? How is the New Creation like a "restart" for the whole world?

3. **Apply:** What is one thing you are excited to do in the New Earth? (Run fast? Eat good food? Hug Jesus?)

If your kid says: "Will I be a ghost in heaven?" **Try:** "No way! Jesus rose with a real body that could eat and touch. We will have real, strong bodies that never get sick or tired."

If your kid says: "I'm scared of the world ending." **Try:** "The end of this broken world is actually the beginning of the perfect world. It's like the end of being sick and the start of feeling great."

BLOCK 4: PRACTICE (One Habit This Week)

One Habit: The "No More" List Read Revelation 21:4. Make a list of things that won't be in the New Earth (No bee stings, no cancer, no fighting, no nightmares).

When we'll do it: Before bed.

What to watch for: Feel the relief that bad things have an expiration date.

Prayer Jesus, come quickly! We can't wait for the day when You make all things new. Help us to live with hope while we wait. Amen.

BLOCK 5: PARENT NOTES (The Secret Weapon)

The Doctrine: Eschatology (New Creation) Biblical hope is not just "going to heaven when we die." It is the bodily resurrection and the restoration of the cosmos. God will unite heaven and earth (Rev 21-22). We will live on a renewed earth, engaging in work, worship, and community without the curse of sin.

Why it matters

- **Physicality:** It affirms that our bodies and the physical world are good (God created them) and worth redeeming.

- **Motivation:** We care for the earth and our communities now because they matter to God's future.

Common Misunderstanding to Avoid

- **Misunderstanding:** The "Floaty Cloud" Error: Thinking heaven is sitting on a cloud playing a harp forever.

    ◦ **Correction:** It will be a vibrant city/garden with activity and joy.

- **Misunderstanding:** The "Escape" Error: Thinking salvation is just escaping earth.

    ◦ **Correction:** Salvation is the redemption of the whole person and creation.

How to Answer Follow-Up Questions

- **Q: Will my dog be there?**

  - A: "The Bible doesn't say for sure, but it does say there will be animals (lions, lambs). God loves His creation, so I wouldn't be surprised!"

- **Q: Will we be bored?**

  - A: "Never. God is infinite. There will always be new things to explore, learn, and do."

Extra Bible anchors for parents Isaiah 11:6–9; Romans 8:19–23; 1 Corinthians 15:42–44.

Teach-it-back prompt "What is the New Creation?"

MEMORY (One-Liner + Catechism Q/A)

One-Line Definition The New Creation is the future world where God fixes everything and lives with us forever.

Q/A Q: What will the New Earth be like? **A:** There will be no more sin, sadness, or death.

Notes:

WEEK 49: REVIEW: THE BIG STORY ENDING

BLOCK 1: KID PAGE (Big Idea + Anchor Verse)

Big Idea The Bible tells one Big Story that moves from Creation to the Fall, through Jesus' rescue, and finally to the Restoration of all things. Right now, we live in the middle of that story as we wait for Jesus to fix the world. Our job is to show people a sneak peek of God's love and tell them the good news.

Anchor Verse *1 Corinthians 15:58* **In kid words:** So, my dear family, stand strong. Let nothing move you. Always give yourself fully to the work of the Lord, because you know that your work for Him is never wasted.

Key Words

- **Creation -> Fall -> Redemption -> Restoration:** The four chapters of the Bible's Big Story.

- **Preview:** Showing people what God's kingdom is like by our actions.

- **Faithfulness:** Sticking with Jesus and doing good until the very end.

More Bible places to look: Micah 6:8; Matthew 25:34–40; Galatians 6:9; Revelation 22:12–13.

BLOCK 2: STORY PAGE (Real Life Scenario)

Story Title: The Neighborhood Mess **Setting:** The local park/playground.

The Story The park down the street was a mess. There was trash under the slide and weeds growing through the swing set. "It's gross," Lucas said. "Let's go somewhere else." His older sister, Mia, stopped. "Wait. We learned that Christians are supposed to care about where they live. Like a preview of heaven, right?" Lucas rolled his eyes. "Picking up candy wrappers isn't heaven." "Maybe not," Mia said, grabbing a discarded cup. "But leaving it messy isn't good either." They spent 20 minutes picking up trash. A lady walking her dog stopped. "Wow, thank you! It looks so much better." Lucas looked at the clean grass. He felt proud.

The Choice Lucas could ignore the mess because "it's not my problem," or he could bring a little bit of order and beauty to his corner of the world.

Resolution "It's not perfect," Lucas said, wiping his hands. "But it's better." "That's the job," Mia smiled. "Making things better until Jesus comes."

Takeaway When we do good work and help others, we show the world a tiny picture of God's future Kingdom.

BLOCK 3: TALK-IT-OUT (Discussion + Coaching)

1. **Understand:** What are the four parts of the Big Story? (Creation, Fall, Redemption, Restoration).

2. **Connect:** How was picking up trash like "Restoration"? (It was taking something messy and making it nice again).

3. **Apply:** What is a small project we can do this week to make our home or neighborhood better?

If your kid says: "My work doesn't matter." **Try:** "Everything matters to God. Even giving a cup of cold water in His name counts."

If your kid says: "I want to skip to the end." **Try:** "We all do! But God has put us here right now for a reason. He has work for you to do today."

BLOCK 4: PRACTICE (One Habit This Week)

One Habit: The Service Project Pick one small thing to fix or clean up in your neighborhood or house (weed a flowerbed, clean the car, bake cookies for a neighbor).

When we'll do it: Saturday morning.

What to watch for: Do it cheerfully, "as unto the Lord."

Prayer Lord, thank You for the Big Story. Thank You that You win in the end. Help me to work hard and love people while I wait for You. Amen.

BLOCK 5: PARENT NOTES (The Secret Weapon)

The Doctrine: Kingdom of God (Already/Not Yet) We live in the tension of the "Already" and the "Not Yet." The Kingdom has come in Jesus (sin is defeated, we are saved), but it is not yet fully here (sickness and death still exist). Our role is to live as citizens of the coming Kingdom now, bringing its values (justice, mercy, beauty) into the present.

Why it matters

- **Perspective:** It gives dignity to our daily work. Cleaning, building, and creating are Kingdom activities.

- **Patience:** It explains why life is still hard. We haven't reached the finish line yet.

Common Misunderstanding to Avoid

- **Misunderstanding:** The "Huddle" Error: Thinking we should just hide in church until Jesus comes.

  - **Correction**: We are called to be salt and light in the world.

- **Misunderstanding:** The "Fix-It-All" Error: Thinking we can bring heaven on earth by ourselves.

  - **Correction**: Only Jesus can fully restore the world. We just point to Him.

How to Answer Follow-Up Questions

- **Q: Does God care about my LEGOs or my drawing?**

  - A: "Yes! He is the Creator. When you create things and enjoy them, you are being like Him."

- **Q: When will the story end?**

  - A: "Only the Father knows the day or hour. But we know it has a happy ending."

Extra Bible anchors for parents Matthew 6:10; Matthew 13:31–32; Colossians 3:23–24.

Teach-it-back prompt "What are the four parts of the Big Story? (Start with Creation...)"

MEMORY (One-Liner + Catechism Q/A)

One-Line Definition We are part of God's Big Story: He made us, He saved us, and He is coming back to fix everything.

Q/A Q: What is our job while we wait for Jesus? **A:** To love God, love our neighbors, and share the Good News.

Notes:

WEEK 50: LIFE SKILL: MAKING WISE CHOICES

BLOCK 1: KID PAGE (Big Idea + Anchor Verse)

Big Idea We make hundreds of choices every day, from picking a shirt to choosing our friends. Wisdom is the skill of making choices that agree with God's way, not just doing what is easy or popular. It is asking, 'What is the right thing to do?' and having the courage to do it.

Anchor Verse *Proverbs 3:5–6* **In kid words:** Trust in the Lord with all your heart. Do not rely on your own understanding. In all your ways, look to Him, and He will make your path straight.

Key Words

- **Wisdom:** Knowing the right thing to do and doing it.

- **Discernment:** Being able to tell the difference between truth and a lie, or safe and dangerous.

- **Peer Pressure:** Feeling pushed to do what everyone else is doing.

More Bible places to look: Psalm 119:105; Proverbs 1:7; Proverbs 13:20; James 1:5; Ephesians 5:15–17.

BLOCK 2: STORY PAGE (Real Life Scenario)

Story Title: The Viral Challenge **Setting:** School lunch table, looking at a phone.

The Story "Look at this!" Jaden held up his phone. A video showed a kid swallowing a spoonful of something spicy and coughing uncontrollably. "It's the Fire Spoon Challenge. Everyone is doing it. We should do it at recess." Two other boys nodded. "Yeah! Let's do it." Alex felt a knot in his stomach. He knew that challenge could make you really sick. His mom had even warned him about it. "Come on, Alex," Jaden said. "Don't be scared." Alex looked at the screen. It looked dumb, honestly. But he didn't want Jaden to think he was a baby. *Think,* Alex told himself. *Is this wise?* "Nah," Alex said, opening his lunchbox. "That looks gross. I'm good."

The Choice Alex could follow the crowd into something stupid, or he could use wisdom to stay safe.

Resolution Jaden shrugged. "Whatever." At recess, Jaden tried it. He ended up throwing up and having to go to the nurse. Alex felt bad for him, but glad he hadn't followed.

Takeaway Wisdom means choosing God's way (and common sense) even when the crowd chooses something else.

<u>BLOCK 3: TALK-IT-OUT (Discussion + Coaching)</u>

1. **Understand:** What is the difference between "knowledge" (knowing facts) and "wisdom" (making good choices)?

2. **Connect:** Have you ever felt pressured to do something silly or unsafe just because friends were doing it?

3. **Apply:** If you aren't sure if a choice is wise, who can you ask? (Parents, Bible, Holy Spirit).

If your kid says: "But everyone is doing it!" **Try:** "I know it feels that way. But 'everyone' can be wrong. God wants you to be a leader who thinks for yourself, not a follower who jumps off a cliff."

If your kid says: "How do I know what God wants?" **Try:** "Ask these three questions: Does the Bible say it's wrong? Is it safe/kind? What do my parents say?"

<u>BLOCK 4: PRACTICE (One Habit This Week)</u>

One Habit: The "Pause Button" This week, when you have to make a tricky choice, hit an imaginary "Pause Button." Count to five and ask, "Is this wise?"

When we'll do it: When buying something, choosing a game, or acting silly.

What to watch for: See if pausing helps you avoid a mistake.

Prayer God, give me wisdom. Help me to trust You more than I trust myself. When I feel pressure to do wrong, give me the strength to stand firm. Amen.

<u>BLOCK 5: PARENT NOTES (The Secret Weapon)</u>

The Doctrine: Wisdom & Christian Ethics Biblical wisdom (*hokmah*) is the "art of skillful living." It begins with the "fear of the Lord" (reverence/respect). We are teaching our kids not just to follow rules, but to develop discernment, the internal compass that aligns with God's character.

Why it matters

- **Independence:** We won't always be there to tell them what to do. They need an internal guide.

- **Safety:** Wisdom protects them from physical and spiritual harm.

Common Misunderstanding to Avoid

- **Misunderstanding:** The "Rule-Follower" Error: Thinking wisdom is just obeying a list.

  - **Correction**: Wisdom is applying God's truth to complex situations.

- **Misunderstanding:** The "Smart Kid" Error: Thinking high grades equals wisdom.

  - **Correction**: You can be a genius and still make foolish life choices.

How to Answer Follow-Up Questions

- **Q: Why are my friends doing bad things?**

    ◦ A: "Sometimes people seek attention or fun without thinking about the cost. We can pray for them to have wisdom."

- Q: Is it a sin to do "neutral thing?"

    ◦ A: "It might not be a 'sin,' but ask: Is it helpful? Is it wise? Does it help you love God?"

Extra Bible anchors for parents Proverbs 4:5–7; Matthew 7:24–27; Colossians 1:9.

Teach-it-back prompt "What did Alex do in the story when he felt pressured?"

MEMORY (One-Liner + Catechism Q/A)

One-Line Definition Wisdom is knowing what is true and right, and choosing to do it.

Q/A Q: Where does wisdom begin? **A:** The fear of the Lord is the beginning of wisdom.

Notes:

WEEK 51: LIFE SKILL: FAITH IN THE REAL WORLD

BLOCK 1: KID PAGE (Big Idea + Anchor Verse)

Big Idea Being a Christian matters just as much on a Tuesday at school as it does on a Sunday at church. God calls us to be 'Salt and Light,' which means we stop bad things from spreading and shine truth in the dark. We show our faith by speaking up for what is right and showing kindness even when others are mean.

Anchor Verse *Micah 6:8* **In kid words:** The Lord has told you what is good. And this is what He requires of you: to do what is right, to love mercy, and to walk humbly with your God.

Key Words

- **Integrity:** Being the same person in public and in private.

- **Courage:** Doing the right thing even when you are scared.

- **Witness:** Showing Jesus to others by how you act.

More Bible places to look: Matthew 5:13–16; Romans 12:21; Ephesians 4:25; Ephesians 4:29; Titus 2:7–8.

BLOCK 2: STORY PAGE (Real Life Scenario)

Story Title: The Group Chat **Setting:** At home, looking at a tablet.

The Story Tyler's tablet dinged. It was the class group chat. Someone posted a funny picture of a girl in their class, Sarah. But then the comments started. "She looks like a troll." "Nobody likes her." "Loser." Tyler felt sick. He knew Sarah. She was quiet and nice. He watched the messages pile up. Everyone was laughing. Tyler wanted to close the app and ignore it. *If I say something, they might turn on me,* he thought. But he remembered the verse: *Do what is right. Love mercy.* His fingers shook as he typed. "Guys, stop. This is mean. Sarah is nice." He hit send. Silence. Then one kid replied: "Yeah, Tyler's right. Cut it out."

The Choice Tyler could be a silent bystander, or he could be a voice of kindness.

Resolution The teasing stopped. Tyler breathed a sigh of relief. He realized that sometimes, one person standing up gives others courage to do the right thing too.

Takeaway Faith in the real world means having the courage to speak the truth in love.

BLOCK 3: TALK-IT-OUT (Discussion + Coaching)

1. **Understand:** What does "do justice" and "love mercy" look like in a group chat?

2. **Connect:** Have you ever seen someone being bullied (online or in person)? What did you do?

3. **Apply:** Is there a situation right now where you need courage to do the right thing?

If your kid says: "It's not my business." **Try:** "God makes justice our business. If we see someone getting hurt and do nothing, we are helping the bully."

If your kid says: "I'm afraid I'll lose my friends." **Try:** "Real friends respect courage. And even if they leave, you have a Friend in Jesus who stands with you."

BLOCK 4: PRACTICE (One Habit This Week)

One Habit: The "Kindness Bomb" Find someone who gets ignored or teased (at school or online). Go out of your way to say something nice to them or sit with them.

When we'll do it: At lunch or recess.

What to watch for: See how they light up when they are treated with dignity.

Prayer Lord, help me to be brave. When I see mean things happening, give me the words to stop it. Help me to act like a Christian everywhere I go. Amen.

BLOCK 5: PARENT NOTES (The Secret Weapon)

The Doctrine: Christian Ethics (Salt & Light) We are called to distinctiveness. We live *in* the world but are not *of* it (John 17). This means our ethical standards come from God, not the culture. We are to be a preserving influence (stopping the decay of kindness/truth) and a revealing influence (shining light on Christ).

Why it matters

- **Witness:** The world judges Jesus by how His followers act.

- **Conscience:** Developing a tender conscience now helps them navigate bigger ethical dilemmas later (work, relationships, politics).

Common Misunderstanding to Avoid

- **Misunderstanding:** The "Bubble" Error: Removing kids from the world so they never face hard choices.

  - **Correction:** They need to learn to swim with a lifeguard (you) nearby.

- **Misunderstanding:** The "Chameleon" Error: Acting like a Christian at church but like the world at school.

  - **Correction:** Integrity is wholeness, being one person everywhere.

How to Answer Follow-Up Questions

- **Q: Why are people so mean online?**

  - A: "Screens make us forget there is a real person with feelings on the other side. We have to remember everyone is made in God's image."

- **Q: What if I get bullied for being nice?**

  - A: "That hurts. But Jesus said, 'Blessed are you when people insult you.' It means you are doing something right."

Extra Bible anchors for parents Proverbs 31:8–9; Matthew 7:12; Galatians 6:10.

Teach-it-back prompt "What did Tyler do in the group chat that was brave?"

MEMORY (One-Liner + Catechism Q/A)

One-Line Definition We show our faith by doing what is right and loving others, even when it's hard.

Q/A Q: What does the Lord require of us? **A:** To do justice, love mercy, and walk humbly with God.

Notes:

WEEK 52: END TIMES: AGREEMENT & DIFFERENCES

BLOCK 1: KID PAGE (Big Idea + Anchor Verse)

Big Idea The Bible ends with the biggest promise of all: Jesus is coming back to fix our broken world. We don't know exactly when He will arrive, but we know He will return as King to take us to be with Him forever. We can live with joy and hope because we know the story has a happy ending.

Anchor Verse *1 Thessalonians 4:16–17* **In kid words:** The Lord Himself will come down from heaven with a loud command and the trumpet call of God. We will meet the Lord in the air and be with Him forever. Therefore, encourage one another with these words.

Key Words

- **Second Coming:** When Jesus returns to earth to judge sin and save His people.

- **Ready:** Living with faith and love so we are happy (not scared) to see Him.

- **Maranatha:** An old prayer that means, "Come, Lord Jesus!"

More Bible places to look: Matthew 24:36; Matthew 24:42–44; Acts 1:11; Revelation 22:20.

BLOCK 2: STORY PAGE (Real Life Scenario)

Story Title: The Bedtime Question **Setting:** Bedroom, lights out.

The Story It was dark. Dad had just finished reading a book. "Dad?" Noah asked quietly. "Yeah, bud?" "What happens when we die? Is it scary? And when is Jesus coming back?" Dad sat back down on the edge of the bed. He knew Noah was thinking about his grandpa who died last year. "That's a big question," Dad said softly. "It can feel a little scary because we haven't done it before. But for those who love Jesus, it's like walking through a door into the best room in the house." "But when will Jesus come?" Noah asked. "We don't know the date," Dad admitted. "But we know *Him*. We know He is good, and we know He wins. So we don't have to be afraid."

The Choice Noah could lay awake worrying about the unknown, or he could trust the King who holds the future.

Resolution Noah let out a breath. "So it's a good surprise?" "The best surprise," Dad said. "Like Christmas morning, but a million times better."

Takeaway We don't know *when* Jesus is coming, but we know it will be a joyful day for His family.

BLOCK 3: TALK-IT-OUT (Discussion + Coaching)

1. **Understand:** Is Jesus coming back secretly or will everyone see Him? (Acts 1 says He will come back in the same way He left, visibly!)

2. **Connect:** Does thinking about the "End of the World" make you scared or excited? Why?

3. **Apply:** How can we get ready for Jesus? (By loving Him and doing His work today).

If your kid says: "I'm scared of dying." **Try:** "That is very normal. But Jesus held the keys to death so we don't have to stay dead. He promised to hold our hand all the way through."

If your kid says: "I heard people talking about beasts and wars." **Try:** "Some parts of the Bible use picture language that sounds intense. But the main point isn't to scare us; it's to tell us that Jesus beats the bad guys."

BLOCK 4: PRACTICE (One Habit This Week)

One Habit: The "Maranatha" Prayer This is the very last prayer in the Bible.

When we'll do it: As you finish the book!

What to watch for: Say together: "Come, Lord Jesus!" Feel the excitement of inviting the King back.

Prayer Lord Jesus, thank You for this whole year of learning about You. We love You. We trust You. Come back soon and make all things new! Amen.

BLOCK 5: PARENT NOTES (The Secret Weapon)

The Doctrine: The Second Coming (Parousia) The return of Christ is the blessed hope of the Church. He will return personally, visibly, and bodily to judge the living and the dead. While the *fact* of His return is a core essential, the *timing* and *nature of the millennium* are secondary issues where good Christians differ.

Why it matters

- **Urgency:** Knowing the time is short motivates us to share the Gospel.

- **Comfort:** We do not grieve as those without hope. The story ends in victory.

Common Misunderstanding to Avoid

- **Misunderstanding:** The "Date Setter" Error: Trying to predict exactly when He will come.

  ○ **Correction:** Jesus said "no one knows the day or hour."

- **Misunderstanding:** The "Panic" Error: Being terrified of the End Times.

  ○ **Correction:** For the believer, it is a day of redemption (Luke 21:28).

How to Answer Follow-Up Questions

- **Q: What will we do in heaven?**

  - A: "We will rule with Jesus, worship Him, and enjoy the New Earth. It won't be boring!"

- **Q: Why is He taking so long?**

  - A: "Because He is patient. He wants as many people as possible to come to repentance (2 Peter 3:9)."

Extra Bible anchors for parents 1 Thessalonians 4:13–18; Titus 2:13; Revelation 22:12.

Christians Differ Box: End Times

What almost all Christians agree on:

- Jesus is coming back physically and visibly.

- There will be a final judgment of the living and the dead.

- God will create a New Heaven and a New Earth.

- Jesus wins!

Common viewpoints:

- **Premillennial:** Believes Jesus will return *before* a literal 1,000-year reign of peace on earth. (Common in Baptist/Non-denominational churches).

- **Amillennial:** Believes the '1,000 years' is a symbol for the current 'church age' where Jesus reigns from heaven and through His people. He will return once at the very end. (Common in Presbyterian/Lutheran/Anglican churches).

- **Postmillennial:** Believes the Gospel will spread and the world will get better and better until Jesus returns *after* a long era of peace.

How to be a good Christian about it: We don't fight over charts and timelines. We simply agree to "watch and be ready." Whether Jesus comes tomorrow or in a thousand years, our job is the same: trust and obey.

Teach-it-back prompt "What is the very last prayer in the Bible? (Come, Lord Jesus!)"

MEMORY (One-Liner + Catechism Q/A)

One-Line Definition We wait with hope for the day Jesus returns to fix the world forever.

Q/A Q: Will Jesus come back? **A:** Yes, He will come again to judge the living and the dead.

Notes:

Conclusion or "The End"

The End of the Beginning

If you are reading this page, take a deep breath. **You did it.**

Maybe it took you exactly 52 weeks of steady, rhythmic reading. Maybe it took you two years of starting and stopping. Maybe your copy of this book is now stained with coffee, dog-eared, or missing a page because a toddler got ahold of it. Maybe you skipped a few weeks when the flu hit your house, or you feel guilty because you didn't do it 'perfectly.' Let that go.

It doesn't matter how you got here. What matters is that you showed up. In a world that constantly pulls families apart, you fought for time to sit down and look at God together. That victory counts.

You Planted Seeds

Over the last year, you have planted seeds in the soil of your child's heart, seeds that will matter for the rest of their lives.

- You planted **Truth** when you opened the Bible and showed them it is a compass, not just a dusty book of rules.

- You planted **Awe** when you talked about God's holiness and helped them see that He is bigger and better than they imagined.

- You planted **Peace** when you talked about Justification, teaching them that they don't have to perform to earn God's love.

- You planted **Hope** when you talked about the New Creation, giving them a happy ending that makes the scary parts of life bearable.

Right now, you might not see a forest. You might look at your kids and still see squirming, eye-rolling, or forgetfulness. You might wonder if anything actually sank in. That is normal. Farmers don't plant a seed and expect to climb a tree the next day. Roots often grow deep in the dark long before green shoots show up in the sun. Discipleship is slow work. It is a long obedience in the same direction.

But know this: **God is the Gardener.** You were faithful to scatter the seed; you can trust the Holy Spirit to water it, protect it, and bring the growth in His perfect timing.

What Now?

This book is finished, but your job isn't. Theology isn't a class you graduate from; it's a relationship you grow into deeper every year.

1. Keep the Conversation Going Don't let the "Kitchen Table" talk stop just because you ran out of chapters. You have built a new muscle; keep using it. When you watch a movie, ask, *"Who is the hero here, and how are they like (or unlike) Jesus?"* When you lose your temper and have to say sorry, remind them, *"This is why I need Jesus just as much as you do."* Keep praying the simple, honest prayers we practiced.

2. Return to the Basics The truths in this book, Creation, Fall, Redemption, Restoration, are the story of your life. Come back to them. You never outgrow the Gospel. Remind your kids (and yourself) every single day that you are sinners saved by grace, loved by the Father, and empowered by the Spirit.

3. Trust the King We ended this year looking at the Return of Jesus. Remember that you are parenting between two advents. Jesus has come, and He is coming again. You don't have to parent in your own strength. In the meantime, He has given you His Spirit to help you parent with courage, kindness, and grace.

A Final Blessing

Parents, never forget that you are the most important theologian in your child's life. You don't need a seminary degree; you just need a sincere faith and a willingness to speak. God chose *you* for *your* kids, not because you are perfect, but because you are His. He knew exactly what He was doing.

May your home be a place where questions are safe, where grace is real, and where Jesus is King.

Well done, good and faithful servant. Now, go have some dinner.

The End

Glossary or "Words I Don't Remember"

This glossary is here so kids can quickly review the "big words" we learned, and so parents have a one-sentence, more precise definition when they want it.

Format: Term → In Kid Words → Parent Note → Where it shows up (Week #s)

Accepted - In Kid Words: Being welcomed and loved just as you are. - **Parent Note:** In Christ, believers are received by God as His children, not on performance, but on grace. - **Where it shows up:** Week 26

Adoption - In Kid Words: A father's legal decision. God brings us into His family and gives us His name. - **Parent Note:** God legally and lovingly brings believers into His family with full rights as sons and daughters in Christ. - **Where it shows up:** Week 31

Advent - In Kid Words: The season leading up to Christmas when we remember Jesus came and will come again. - **Parent Note:** The church season that anticipates and celebrates Christ's coming, His first coming and His promised return. - **Where it shows up:** Week 51

Affection - In Kid Words: Showing love through attention, hugs, or kind words. - **Parent Note:** More precisely: Showing love through attention, hugs, or kind words. - **Where it shows up:** Week 12

Affirmation - In Kid Words: Using words to build someone up. - **Parent Note:** More precisely: Using words to build someone up. - **Where it shows up:** Week 12

Amen - In Kid Words: A word that means "yes, that's true" or "let it be so." - **Parent Note:** More precisely: A word that means "yes, that's true" or "let it be so." - **Where it shows up:** Week 39

Anchor Verse - In Kid Words: The main Bible verse for the week. - **Parent Note:** More precisely: The main Bible verse for the week. - **Where it shows up:** Week 1

Atonement - In Kid Words: Jesus taking our place so we can be forgiven. - **Parent Note:** Christ's saving work that removes sin and restores sinners to God through His life, death, and resurrection. - **Where it shows up:** Week 29

Authority - In Kid Words: The right to say what's true and what's right. - **Parent Note:** God's rightful rule; in Scripture, authority rests in God's Word and is exercised under Him, not above Him. - **Where it shows up:** Week 2

Baptism - In Kid Words: A sign of belonging to Jesus and His people. - **Parent Note:** The covenant sign of entry into the visible church, marking union with Christ and cleansing signified by water. - **Where it shows up:** Week 41

Belief - In Kid Words: Thinking something is true. - **Parent Note:** More precisely: Thinking something is true. - **Where it shows up:** Week 6

Blessing - In Kid Words: God's good gift. - **Parent Note:** More precisely: God's good gift. - **Where it shows up:** Week 9

Body - In Kid Words: The people of the church together. - **Parent Note:** More precisely: The people of the church together. - **Where it shows up:** Week 45

Boldness - In Kid Words: Courage to do what's right even when it's hard. - **Parent Note:** A Christian virtue of courage to do what's right even when it's hard. - **Where it shows up:** Week 6

Born Again - In Kid Words: God giving you a new heart that loves Him. - **Parent Note:** More precisely: God giving you a new heart that loves Him. - **Where it shows up:** Week 32

Breath Prayer - In Kid Words: A short prayer you can whisper in one breath. - **Parent Note:** More precisely: A short prayer you can whisper in one breath. - **Where it shows up:** Week 5

Catechism - In Kid Words: A question-and-answer tool that helps you learn the faith. - **Parent Note:** More precisely: A question-and-answer tool that helps you learn the faith. - **Where it shows up:** Week 1

Character - In Kid Words: The kind of person you are becoming. - **Parent Note:** Moral and spiritual integrity shaped by what we love and repeatedly choose. - **Where it shows up:** Week 6

Comfort - In Kid Words: Help and peace when you're hurting. - **Parent Note:** A Christian virtue of help and peace when you're hurting. - **Where it shows up:** Week 47

Communion - In Kid Words: A church meal where we remember Jesus' death and celebrate His love. - **Parent Note:** The Lord's Supper, Christ's covenant meal for the church, signifying and strengthening communion with Him and His people. - **Where it shows up:** Week 42

Communion of Saints - In Kid Words: The special bond Christians share as one family in Jesus. - **Parent Note:** The spiritual union and shared life believers have with Christ and with one another across time and place. - **Where it shows up:** Week 45

Compassion - In Kid Words: Caring about someone's pain and wanting to help. - **Parent Note:** A Christian virtue of caring about someone's pain and wanting to help. - **Where it shows up:** Week 14, 47

Confess - In Kid Words: Telling God the truth about your sin. - **Parent Note:** To agree with God about our sin and bring it into the light, trusting His forgiveness in Christ. - **Where it shows up:** Week 33

Contentment - In Kid Words: Being thankful and at peace with what you have. - **Parent Note:** A Christian virtue of being thankful and at peace with what you have. - **Where it shows up:** Week 34

Context - In Kid Words: What comes before and after a verse. - **Parent Note:** The literary and historical setting that governs meaning when interpreting Scripture. - **Where it shows up:** Week 3

Conversion - In Kid Words: Turning to God with faith. - **Parent Note:** The Spirit-worked turning to God that includes repentance and faith. - **Where it shows up:** Week 33

Courage - In Kid Words: Doing the right thing even when you feel afraid. - **Parent Note:** A Christian virtue of doing the right thing even when you feel afraid. - **Where it shows up:** Week 34

Covenant - In Kid Words: A strong promise that creates a family relationship. - **Parent Note:** A binding relationship God establishes (by promise) that defines His people's identity, blessings, and responsibilities. - **Where it shows up:** Week 25

Creation - In Kid Words: God making everything. - **Parent Note:** More precisely: God making everything. - **Where it shows up:** Week 9

Creation → Fall → Redemption → Restoration - In Kid Words: The big story of the Bible in four parts. - **Parent Note:** A four-part biblical storyline summarizing redemptive history: God creates, sin breaks, Christ redeems, and God restores all things. - **Where it shows up:** Week 9

Creator - In Kid Words: God as the Maker of all things. - **Parent Note:** God as the sovereign Maker of all that exists, distinct from and Lord over His creation. - **Where it shows up:** Week 9

Curiosity - In Kid Words: Wanting to learn more by asking good questions. - **Parent Note:** More precisely: Wanting to learn more by asking good questions. - **Where it shows up:** Week 1

Curse - In Kid Words: The brokenness that comes because of sin. - **Parent Note:** The just judgment of God on sin, death and disorder, reversing the blessing of Eden. - **Where it shows up:** Week 10

Day 4 Habit - In Kid Words: A small weekly practice to build a strong faith. - **Parent Note:** More precisely: A small weekly practice to build a strong faith. - **Where it shows up:** Week 1

Discernment - In Kid Words: Knowing what's true and what's not. - **Parent Note:** A Christian virtue of knowing what's true and what's not. - **Where it shows up:** Week 2

Disciple - In Kid Words: A learner and follower of Jesus. - **Parent Note:** More precisely: A learner and follower of Jesus. - **Where it shows up:** Week 6

Discipline - In Kid Words: Doing what's right even when you don't feel like it. - **Parent Note:** More precisely: Doing what's right even when you don't feel like it. - **Where it shows up:** Week 43

Doctrine - In Kid Words: A clear teaching about God from the Bible. - **Parent Note:** A settled teaching drawn from Scripture that helps the church believe, worship, and live faithfully. - **Where it shows up:** Week 1

Doubt - In Kid Words: Feeling unsure if something is true. - **Parent Note:** More precisely: Feeling unsure if something is true. - **Where it shows up:** Week 7

Doxology - In Kid Words: Words or songs that praise God. - **Parent Note:** More precisely: Words or songs that praise God. - **Where it shows up:** Week 35

Dignity - In Kid Words: Your worth as someone made by God. - **Parent Note:** A Christian virtue of your worth as someone made by God. - **Where it shows up:** Week 8

Divine - In Kid Words: Something that belongs to God. - **Parent Note:** What belongs to God's nature, His being, attributes, and works as God. - **Where it shows up:** Week 27

Ecclesiology - In Kid Words: The part of theology that studies the church, what it is and what it's for. - **Parent Note:** The doctrine of the church, its nature, marks, mission, and ordered life under Christ. - **Where it shows up:** Week 45

End Times - In Kid Words: What God says will happen in the future. - **Parent Note:** More precisely: What God says will happen in the future. - **Where it shows up:** Week 52

Escape Route - In Kid Words: A smart plan to get away from temptation. - **Parent Note:** God-provided ways to endure temptation, truth, prayer, wise choices, and practical steps that remove opportunity. - **Where it shows up:** Week 50

Eschatology - In Kid Words: The part of theology that studies the "last things", Jesus' return and the future God promised. - **Parent Note:** The doctrine of last things, Christ's return, resurrection, judgment, and the consummation of the kingdom. - **Where it shows up:** Week 52

Eternal Life - In Kid Words: Life with God forever. - **Parent Note:** More precisely: Life with God forever. - **Where it shows up:** Week 1

Evangelism - In Kid Words: Sharing the good news about Jesus. - **Parent Note:** The loving proclamation of the gospel that calls people to repent and believe in Jesus. - **Where it shows up:** Week 46

Ex Nihilo - In Kid Words: "Out of nothing." God created without using pre-existing materials. - **Parent Note:** Creation "out of nothing", God brought all things into being by His Word and power, not from pre-existing matter. - **Where it shows up:** Week 9

Faith - In Kid Words: Trusting God even when you can't see. - **Parent Note:** Trusting, receiving, and resting on Christ, personally relying on God's promises rather than our own goodness. - **Where it shows up:** Week 4, 7

Faithfulness - In Kid Words: Staying steady and true over time. - **Parent Note:** A Christian virtue of staying steady and true over time. - **Where it shows up:** Week 19

Fiducia - In Kid Words: A fancy word for trust, leaning your whole weight on God because He is solid. - **Parent Note:** A Latin term emphasizing faith as personal trust and reliance, not mere assent or optimism. - **Where it shows up:** Week 4

Fides qua - In Kid Words: Latin for "the faith by which we believe", the trusting heart (the act). - **Parent Note:** The subjective act of believing, the trust by which a person embraces Christ and His promises. - **Where it shows up:** Week 7

Fides quae - In Kid Words: Latin for "the faith we believe", the truths about God (the content). - **Parent Note:** The objective content of Christian belief, the doctrines confessed by the church. - **Where it shows up:** Week 7

Fides quaerens intellectum - In Kid Words: A Latin phrase that means "faith seeking understanding", we trust God and keep asking questions to learn more. - **Parent Note:** A classic Christian motto meaning faith seeks deeper understanding through humble inquiry. - **Where it shows up:** Week 7

Forgive - In Kid Words: Letting go of revenge and showing mercy. - **Parent Note:** A spiritual practice of letting go of revenge and showing mercy. - **Where it shows up:** Week 33

Fruit of the Spirit - In Kid Words: The good qualities the Holy Spirit grows in us. - **Parent Note:** More precisely: The good qualities the Holy Spirit grows in us. - **Where it shows up:** Week 37

Gathering - In Kid Words: Meeting with other believers to worship. - **Parent Note:** A spiritual practice of meeting with other believers to worship. - **Where it shows up:** Week 45

Genre - In Kid Words: A type of writing, like poetry or history. - **Parent Note:** More precisely: A type of writing, like poetry or history. - **Where it shows up:** Week 3

Glorification - In Kid Words: When God finishes making us fully like Jesus. - **Parent Note:** The final stage of salvation when believers are fully made like Christ in resurrected glory. - **Where it shows up:** Week 48

Glory - In Kid Words: God's greatness on display. - **Parent Note:** More precisely: God's greatness on display. - **Where it shows up:** Week 23

Gospel - In Kid Words: The good news that Jesus saves. - **Parent Note:** The good news that Jesus is Lord and Savior, He lived, died, and rose to save sinners who repent and believe. - **Where it shows up:** Week 29, 46

Grace - In Kid Words: God giving us good gifts we don't deserve. - **Parent Note:** God's undeserved favor and help given to sinners in Christ, both His saving kindness and His empowering strength. - **Where it shows up:** Week 26, 30

Gratitude - In Kid Words: Saying "thank you" with your words and your life. - **Parent Note:** A Christian virtue of saying "thank you" with your words and your life. - **Where it shows up:** Week 36

Habits - In Kid Words: Small repeated actions that shape who you become. - **Parent Note:** More precisely: Small repeated actions that shape who you become. - **Where it shows up:** Week 1

Hallelujah - In Kid Words: A word that means "Praise the Lord!" - **Parent Note:** A spiritual practice of a word that means "Praise the Lord!" - **Where it shows up:** Week 35

Hermeneutics - In Kid Words: The skill of interpreting the Bible carefully so we understand what God meant. - **Parent Note:** The principles and practice of interpreting Scripture according to authorial intent, genre, and context. - **Where it shows up:** Week 3

Holy - In Kid Words: Set apart, perfectly pure. - **Parent Note:** More precisely: Set apart, perfectly pure. - **Where it shows up:** Week 11

Hope - In Kid Words: Looking forward with confidence because of God's promises. - **Parent Note:** A Christian virtue of looking forward with confidence because of God's promises. - **Where it shows up:** Week 47, 49

Humility - In Kid Words: Not thinking too highly of yourself. - **Parent Note:** A Christian virtue of not thinking too highly of yourself. - **Where it shows up:** Week 36

Hypostatic Union - In Kid Words: A term that says Jesus is one Person with two natures, fully God and fully man. - **Parent Note:** The doctrine that the one Person of Christ exists in two natures, divine and human, without confusion or division. - **Where it shows up:** Week 28

Identity - In Kid Words: Who you are and what's most true about you. - **Parent Note:** A Christian virtue of who you are and what's most true about you. - **Where it shows up:** Week 8

Image of God - In Kid Words: Humans are made to reflect God. - **Parent Note:** Humanity's unique dignity and calling to reflect God's character, represent His rule, and relate to Him and others. - **Where it shows up:** Week 8

Incarnation - In Kid Words: God the Son becoming a real human. - **Parent Note:** The Son of God took on a true human nature, Jesus is fully God and fully man in one Person. - **Where it shows up:** Week 28

Indwelling - In Kid Words: God living in us by His Spirit. - **Parent Note:** The Spirit's abiding presence in believers, uniting them to Christ and empowering holiness. - **Where it shows up:** Week 37

Inspiration - In Kid Words: God guiding the Bible's writers so the Bible is His Word. - **Parent Note:** The Spirit's work by which Scripture is God-breathed, fully God's Word through human authors. - **Where it shows up:** Week 2

Integrity - In Kid Words: Being the same on the inside and outside. - **Parent Note:** A Christian virtue of being the same on the inside and outside. - **Where it shows up:** Week 6

Intercession - In Kid Words: Jesus praying for us. - **Parent Note:** Christ's ongoing priestly work of representing and pleading for His people before the Father. - **Where it shows up:** Week 44

Justification - In Kid Words: God declaring you right with Him because of Jesus. - **Parent Note:** God's legal declaration that a sinner is righteous in His sight because of Christ alone, received by faith alone. - **Where it shows up:** Week 30

Justice - In Kid Words: Doing what's right and fair. - **Parent Note:** More precisely: Doing what's right and fair. - **Where it shows up:** Week 13

Lament - In Kid Words: Telling God you're sad and asking for help. - **Parent Note:** A spiritual practice of telling God you're sad and asking for help. - **Where it shows up:** Week 47

Life Skill - In Kid Words: A helpful habit for everyday life. - **Parent Note:** More precisely: A helpful habit for everyday life. - **Where it shows up:** Week 1

Lie - In Kid Words: Saying something false on purpose. - **Parent Note:** More precisely: Saying something false on purpose. - **Where it shows up:** Week 20

Longsuffering - In Kid Words: Patience that keeps going. - **Parent Note:** More precisely: Patience that keeps going. - **Where it shows up:** Week 21

Love - In Kid Words: Choosing good for someone. - **Parent Note:** More precisely: Choosing good for someone. - **Where it shows up:** Week 12

Maranatha - In Kid Words: "Come, Lord!", a prayer for Jesus to return. - **Parent Note:** More precisely: "Come, Lord!", a prayer for Jesus to return. - **Where it shows up:** Week 52

Maturity - In Kid Words: Growing up spiritually. - **Parent Note:** A Christian virtue of growing up spiritually. - **Where it shows up:** Week 43

Means of Grace - In Kid Words: Ordinary ways God helps us grow (like Bible, prayer, church). - **Parent Note:** The ordinary channels God uses to give and strengthen faith, especially Word, prayer, and sacraments (and the fellowship of the church). - **Where it shows up:** Week 40

Memory - In Kid Words: A short truth to memorize and keep in your heart. - **Parent Note:** More precisely: A short truth to memorize and keep in your heart. - **Where it shows up:** Week 1

Mercy - In Kid Words: Giving kindness when someone deserves punishment. - **Parent Note:** A Christian virtue of giving kindness when someone deserves punishment. - **Where it shows up:** Week 14, 33

Mighty - In Kid Words: Strong and powerful. - **Parent Note:** More precisely: Strong and powerful. - **Where it shows up:** Week 16

Mission - In Kid Words: God's purpose and our part in it. - **Parent Note:** More precisely: God's purpose and our part in it. - **Where it shows up:** Week 46

Name - In Kid Words: A word that tells who someone is. - **Parent Note:** More precisely: A word that tells who someone is. - **Where it shows up:** Week 24

Near - In Kid Words: Close, not far away. - **Parent Note:** More precisely: Close, not far away. - **Where it shows up:** Week 17

Neighbor - In Kid Words: Anyone God puts near you to love. - **Parent Note:** A Christian virtue of anyone God puts near you to love. - **Where it shows up:** Week 47

New Creation - In Kid Words: God's future world where everything is made new. - **Parent Note:** God's promised future where sin and death are gone and everything is made new under Christ's reign. - **Where it shows up:** Week 48

Omnipotent - In Kid Words: All-powerful. - **Parent Note:** More precisely: All-powerful. - **Where it shows up:** Week 16

Omnipresent - In Kid Words: Present everywhere. - **Parent Note:** More precisely: Present everywhere. - **Where it shows up:** Week 17

Omniscient - In Kid Words: Knowing everything. - **Parent Note:** More precisely: Knowing everything. - **Where it shows up:** Week 18

Ordinance/Sacrament - In Kid Words: A church practice Jesus told us to do. - **Parent Note:** A church practice instituted by Christ that serves as a visible sign and seal of gospel promises (terminology varies by tradition). - **Where it shows up:** Week 41

Patience - In Kid Words: Waiting without anger. - **Parent Note:** A Christian virtue of waiting without anger. - **Where it shows up:** Week 21

Peer Pressure - In Kid Words: Feeling pushed to do something because others are doing it. - **Parent Note:** More precisely: Feeling pushed to do something because others are doing it. - **Where it shows up:** Week 50

Petition - In Kid Words: Asking God for help. - **Parent Note:** A spiritual practice of asking God for help. - **Where it shows up:** Week 38

Progress - In Kid Words: Small growth over time. - **Parent Note:** A Christian virtue of small growth over time. - **Where it shows up:** Week 43

Promise - In Kid Words: A word you can count on. - **Parent Note:** More precisely: A word you can count on. - **Where it shows up:** Week 19, 25

Providence - In Kid Words: God guiding and caring for everything. - **Parent Note:** God's wise and loving governance of all things, preserving, directing, and providing for His creation. - **Where it shows up:** Week 44

Prayer - In Kid Words: Talking to God. - **Parent Note:** Communion with God, speaking and listening in relationship, in Jesus' name, by the Spirit, according to God's will. - **Where it shows up:** Week 38

Ready - In Kid Words: Prepared, not panicking. - **Parent Note:** A Christian virtue of prepared, not panicking. - **Where it shows up:** Week 49

Regeneration - In Kid Words: God giving you a new heart. - **Parent Note:** The Spirit's act of giving new spiritual life, being "born again," creating faith and repentance. - **Where it shows up:** Week 32

Repentance - In Kid Words: Turning away from sin and back to God. - **Parent Note:** Turning from sin to God with sorrow for sin and a new desire to obey, trusting Christ for forgiveness. - **Where it shows up:** Week 33

Resurrection - In Kid Words: Jesus rising from the dead. - **Parent Note:** God raising Jesus bodily from the dead, securing victory over sin and death and the future resurrection of believers. - **Where it shows up:** Week 48

Review - In Kid Words: Looking back to remember and grow. - **Parent Note:** A spiritual practice of looking back to remember and grow. - **Where it shows up:** Week 6

Righteous - In Kid Words: Right and fair. - **Parent Note:** More precisely: Right and fair. - **Where it shows up:** Week 13

Righteousness - In Kid Words: Doing what is right in God's eyes. - **Parent Note:** Right standing and right living measured by God's holy standard; for believers, a gift in Christ and a growing practice. - **Where it shows up:** Week 30

Sacrament - In Kid Words: A special sign Jesus gave the church. - **Parent Note:** More precisely: A special sign Jesus gave the church. - **Where it shows up:** Week 42

Sanctification - In Kid Words: God helping you grow to be more like Jesus. - **Parent Note:** God's lifelong work of making believers holy, growing us to love what God loves and obey from the heart. - **Where it shows up:** Week 43

Second Coming - In Kid Words: Jesus returning again. - **Parent Note:** Christ's future, bodily, visible return to judge, save, and renew the world. - **Where it shows up:** Week 52

Scripture - In Kid Words: Another name for the Bible. - **Parent Note:** More precisely: Another name for the Bible. - **Where it shows up:** Week 5

Selfless - In Kid Words: Putting others first. - **Parent Note:** A Christian virtue of putting others first. - **Where it shows up:** Week 35

Set Apart - In Kid Words: Different for a special purpose. - **Parent Note:** More precisely: Different for a special purpose. - **Where it shows up:** Week 11

Sin - In Kid Words: Anything we think, say, or do that goes against God. - **Parent Note:** Any failure to live in full love and obedience to God, both wrong actions and the heart's rebellion. - **Where it shows up:** Week 10

Sovereign - In Kid Words: In charge of everything. - **Parent Note:** God's supreme authority and freedom to accomplish His purposes without rival. - **Where it shows up:** Week 44

Stone Heart - In Kid Words: A heart that doesn't love God. - **Parent Note:** A biblical picture of spiritual deadness and stubbornness that needs God's renewing grace (Ezekiel 36). - **Where it shows up:** Week 32

Substitute - In Kid Words: Someone who takes another person's place. - **Parent Note:** Christ taking our place under judgment so we can receive His righteousness and welcome. - **Where it shows up:** Week 29

Sustain - In Kid Words: God holding everything together. - **Parent Note:** God's ongoing care by which He upholds creation and His people moment by moment. - **Where it shows up:** Week 44

Suffering - In Kid Words: Pain and hard things in life. - **Parent Note:** The experience of pain and loss in a fallen world that God uses for His purposes and will one day end. - **Where it shows up:** Week 47

Thanksgiving - In Kid Words: Thanking God on purpose. - **Parent Note:** A spiritual practice of thanking God on purpose. - **Where it shows up:** Week 36

Temptation - In Kid Words: Feeling pulled toward sin. - **Parent Note:** An invitation to sin that appeals to our desires; resisting involves faith, wisdom, and Spirit-enabled obedience. - **Where it shows up:** Week 50

The Body of Christ - In Kid Words: A picture of the church as one body with many parts. - **Parent Note:** A biblical picture of the church as one living body with Christ as the Head and believers as interdependent members. - **Where it shows up:** Week 45

The Fall - In Kid Words: The moment humans first sinned against God. - **Parent Note:** Humanity's first sin and its consequences, alienation from God, corruption, and death entering the world. - **Where it shows up:** Week 10

The Flesh - In Kid Words: The sinful part of us that wants to disobey God. - **Parent Note:** Our sinful nature apart from God, disordered desires that oppose the Spirit. - **Where it shows up:** Week 50

The Lord's Supper - In Kid Words: Another name for communion. - **Parent Note:** Christ's covenant meal for baptized believers that proclaims His death and nourishes faith as we receive with trust. - **Where it shows up:** Week 42

Theology - In Kid Words: Learning who God is and how to live with Him. - **Parent Note:** The study of God and all things in relation to God as He has revealed Himself, especially in Scripture. - **Where it shows up:** Week 1

Training - In Kid Words: Practice that helps you get stronger. - **Parent Note:** Intentional practice aimed at growth; in discipleship, training shapes habits that align our lives with Christ. - **Where it shows up:** Week 43

Trinity - In Kid Words: One God in three Persons: Father, Son, and Holy Spirit. - **Parent Note:** One God in three Persons, Father, Son, and Holy Spirit, equal in deity, distinct in personhood, one in essence. - **Where it shows up:** Week 27

Trust - In Kid Words: Relying on someone. - **Parent Note:** A Christian virtue of relying on someone. - **Where it shows up:** Week 4, 7

Truth - In Kid Words: What's real and right. - **Parent Note:** What is real as God defines it; in Christianity, truth is grounded in God's character and revealed in His Word. - **Where it shows up:** Week 4, 20

Unity - In Kid Words: Being one family even when we are different. - **Parent Note:** A Christian virtue of being one family even when we are different. - **Where it shows up:** Week 45

Weight - In Kid Words: Something heavy (used to explain glory). - **Parent Note:** More precisely: Something heavy (used to explain glory). - **Where it shows up:** Week 23

Witness - In Kid Words: Telling others about what Jesus has done. - **Parent Note:** Telling the truth about Jesus with words and life, pointing others to Him as Savior and Lord. - **Where it shows up:** Week 46

Wise Choices - In Kid Words: Choosing what's right, not what's easy. - **Parent Note:** More precisely: Choosing what's right, not what's easy. - **Where it shows up:** Week 50

Wisdom - In Kid Words: Knowing what to do and doing it. - **Parent Note:** A Christian virtue of knowing what to do and doing it. - **Where it shows up:** Week 1, 15

Worship - In Kid Words: Honoring and loving God with your whole life. - **Parent Note:** Giving God the honor He deserves, our whole-life response of love, awe, obedience, and praise. - **Where it shows up:** Week 35

Yahweh - In Kid Words: God's special name. - **Parent Note:** More precisely: God's special name. - **Where it shows up:** Week 24